THREE POETS OF THE
RHYMERS' CLUB

THREE POETS OF THE RHYMERS' CLUB

Ernest Dowson
Lionel Johnson
John Davidson

selected and introduced by
Derek Stanford

FYFIELD BOOKS
A Carcanet Press Publication

SBN 85635 089 3 – cloth
SBN 85635 090 7 – paper

First published in 1974
by Carcanet Press Ltd
266 Councillor Lane
Cheadle Hulme, Cheadle
Cheshire SK8 5PN

Printed in Great Britain
by W & J Mackay Limited, Chatham

Contents

From *The Pierrot of the Minute* (1897)

From *Decorations* (1899)

MARGARET
Conjugi Dilectissimae

Introduction

1 Ernest Dowson (1867–1900): Life

ERNEST DOWSON was born at Lee to the south-east of London. His mother, a beautiful woman (remembered by one of her son's friends for 'something extraordinarily pathetic in her charming face'[1]) was unstable. Alfred Dowson, a person of some means, was 'a remarkable man, a wit, the friend of half the interesting artists and men of letters of his generation'[2] including Browning and Stevenson. Unfortunately, he was also consumptive.

There is no evidence that Dowson ever attended school, and it is likely that he was instructed by his father. A charming and somewhat sophisticated young man (with a 'wider knowledge of such places as the Paris music hall than most undergraduates possess'[3]) he went up to Oxford in 1888 to read Classics. He came down without completing his papers for Honour Moderations for reasons unknown.

The prime misrepresenter of Dowson's days at Oxford is Arthur Symons, who both knew and admired the poet greatly, but whose persuasive obituary essay (later reprinted as an introduction to many editions of Dowson's poems) includes falsifications of fact, like the statement, 'At Oxford, I believe, his favourite form of intoxication had been haschisch'. Symons believed what would accord with his image of Dowson as 'the modern decadent' with his 'curious love [or affectation] of the sordid'.[4] Dowson's fellow undergraduate, W. R. Thomas, nailed Symons' hashish story: Dowson *had* taken it – three times; but his favourite stimulant at that time was 'chablis and soda'.[5]

John Gawsworth and Sir Desmond Flower (the greatest English authority on Dowson) both over-reacted to Symons' interpretation. Edgar Jepson, who was the poet's friend for two years, admits that, 'As long as I could keep Dowson to wine or beer, he was sober enough. When his nervous irritation drove him to the poisonous juice of the potato there was little to be done.'[6] Absinthe, also, at times

11

took its toll. In fact, constitutional frailty combined in his make-up with a melancholic disposition. Dowson had come up to Oxford with a philosophy of pessimism fully formulated; derived from the writings of Schopenhauer, this reflected his partly depressive nature. A sonnet, written during his Oxford period, speaks of the physically weak idealistic man's dismay at the animal mechanism of nature:

> I know thee, evil one, and I am ware
> Of all thy vileness; – never song of mine
> Shall swell the shameful triumphs that are thine . . . .

Later, when he joined the Roman Church in 1891, his personal philosophy of pessimism became an attitude of resignation.

There is no doubt that Symons' Dowson was one of the critic's apocryphal 'studies in strange souls'. As to Dowson's inveterate womanizing, there are few specific pieces of evidence. Just two years before his death, Oscar Wilde, in a letter to the publisher Smithers, spoke of a 'Mrs Dowson' whom he found boring, but most of the evidence points to a few limited encounters.

Dowson was no sooner down from Oxford than he met the young girl who was to leave him 'idolatrous for the rest of [his] days',[7] since through her he experienced that 'mystery – an absolute absorption in one particular person'.[8] It is clear that this experience was of a quasi-mystical nature – what might be called a Beatrician encounter. Of this experience, he declared to one friend that, 'it reconciles all inconsistencies in the order of things, and . . . above all it seems . . . to reduce to utter absurdity any material explanation of itself or of the world,'[9] and to another, 'I write as an *illuminatio*: I seem to have seen mysteries, and if I fail to be explicit, it is because my eyes are dazzled.'[10]

Adelaide Foltinowicz's father ran the 'Poland' restaurant, near Shaftesbury Avenue. 'Missie' was between twelve and thirteen when Dowson first met her. When she was fifteen he proposed to her, but she regarded him with 'a friendly affection and no deeper feeling'.[11]

In his portrait of the poet, Edgar Jepson tells us that there was a cult of little girls at Oxford; though it should be remembered that this was the age of Lewis Carroll's Alice not Vladimir Nabokov's Lolita. Max Beerbohm professed a devotion to Cissy Loftus – 'The

Mimetic Marvel' – a star of the Tivoli aged fifteen, and Dowson one to Minnie Terry – a child-actress only seven, a collection of whose photographs and souvenirs he possessed. Our age thinks in Freudian terms, but 'Peter-Pan-ery' seems stronger in Dowson than 'nymphetomania'; the poet Victor Plarr remembered his first conversation with him thus:

> 'Shall you ever feel old?'
> 'No; I am static – about four years of age.'[12]

Dowson never recovered from Adelaide's rejection of him. At this time, too, his father's health deteriorated further, partly under the pressure of financial worry, and in August 1894 he died in circumstances which suggested suicide. Six months later, Dowson's mother hanged herself.

From 1895, the poet lived mainly abroad, chiefly in Paris and Brittany. He was now almost wholly dependent on his pen for his living. The publisher Leonard Smithers doled him out a weekly stipend for translation work ('never,' as Symons tells us, 'without some traces of his peculiar quality of charm in language'). Smithers has frequently been presented as Dowson's evil angel. A debauchee of convivial disposition, he liked to revel with his authors. Robert Harborough Sherard speaks of his 'swine-fugues' in pursuit of Parisian 'mud-honey'.[13] Dowson was often his guest-companion – a dangerous honour since he had by then contracted phthisis. But Smithers was also the poet's only patron. In his *Aspects of Wilde* (1936), Vincent O'Sullivan remarked that 'All the verse or prose that Dowson cared to produce, Smithers was ready to publish', including the many poems and stories he printed in *The Savoy*.

It is from these last years that the myth of the unkempt bohemian derives. Gertrude Atherton remembers him at Pont-Aven 'unshaven, his hair . . . long and dusty'; and again, a year or two later, at the Mass for the repose of Aubrey Beardsley in Farm Street 'more like a lost soul than ever as he drifted past with his unseeing eyes'.[14] The pathetic details of his death have been well told by Robert Harborough Sherard – who nursed him for the last six weeks of his life at Catford – in his book *The Real Oscar Wilde*.

2 Ernest Dowson: Work

As Sir Desmond Flower has pointed out, the literary facts of Dowson's life show him to have been 'more hardworking . . . than his detractors thought'.[15] His published work includes two novels, written in collaboration with his friend Arthur Moore: *A Comedy of Masks* (1893) and *Adrian Rome* (1899); a volume of short stories: *Dilemmas* (1895); two volumes of poetry: *Verses* (1896) and *Decorations* (1899); a verse-play: *The Pierrot of the Minute* (1897); and eight or nine volumes of translation. In addition, he contributed articles and reviews to the *Critic*.

Sir Desmond Flower has listed the 'few strings to his poetic bow' namely, 'his ill success in love, the unalterable progress from childhood to womanhood of each unsophisticated creature on whom he set his affections, his disgust with life and mankind when one of these charming children lived up to his worst fears and gradually became sex-conscious and gauche, autumn and the winter of death as the only rest from this *lâcheté*'.[16] Dowson's economy of theme is accompanied by a like economy of effect. He had two aims: purity and fluency of music, and felicity of diction. In a letter to his friend Arthur Moore he spoke of the first criterion, saying that what he sought to offer was 'verses in the manner of the French "symbolists": verses making for mere sound, and music, with just a suggestion of sense or hardly that . . .'.[17]

Some of Verlaine's poems were obviously Dowson's ideal in musicality, and his own magical rendition of four of the French poet's poems in *Decorations* shows his debt. He also admired the *melopoeia* of Edgar Allen Poe, typified in the alliterative virtuosity of 'The viol, the violet, and the vine'. Unlike Swinburne, Dowson aspired to a simplicity of music:

> To my last love
> Loved all above:
> At evening
> Of autumn
> One chrysanthemum
> Is all I have to bring.

Yet Dowson did not publish 'Fantasie Triste', from which this stanza comes, probably regarding it as an exercise in sound.

Dowson has also left on record his devotion to a cult of the epithet. In a letter to his Oxford friend Sam Smith – translator of the *Lysistrata* which Beardsley was to illustrate – he writes: 'I have just read through the VIth "Aeneid"; and I am intoxicated with its adorable phrases. After all, with all our labour of the file and chisel we cannot approach these people, in this gross tongue.'[18] In this same letter, Dowson goes on to admit that 'a Virgilian couplet has inspired him to a poem';[19] and on this assumption – against the opinion of most commentators who associate the inspiration of the 'Cynara' poem directly with Adelaide Foltinowicz – John Gawsworth asks 'Is not the Horatian phrase from the first Ode of the fourth book . . . the sole genesis of "Cynara", as it is its title?' 'The phrase [*non sum qualis eram bonae/sub regno Cinarae*]' he argues, 'excited Dowson's imagination to such a degree that he honoured it with a new poem.'[20] (In this connection, Sir B. Ifor Evans points out that though the mistress in Dowson's poem derives from Horace, 'the situation . . . arises from memories of Propertius' *Cynthia*.'[21])

In his 'memories' of Dowson – whether genuine or fictitious – Frank Harris presents a characteristic image of the poet; during a stroll in Hyde Park, Dowson recited to him, 'in his pleasing pathetic tenor voice' – 'the slight, stooping figure and the liquid appealing eye, framed by a bed of crimson flowers'[22] – his thin hands twisted as he spoke the words – the poem 'Sapientia Lunae':

> The wisdom of the world said unto me:
> *'Go forth and run, the race is to the brave;*
> *Perchance some honour tarrieth for thee!'*
> 'As tarrieth,' I said, 'for sure, the grave.'
> For I had pondered on a rune of roses,
> Which to her votaries the moon discloses.

It is because his poems effect a distillation of their author's drama, with 'uncomplaining almost stoical independence'[23] of manner, that their apparent slightness is deceptive. Few writers have so nicely matched their resources and their production. 'He knew his limits only too well,'[24] wrote Symons – too well, that is, ever to overstep them.

15

3 Lionel Johnson (1867–1902): Life

Lionel Johnson, youngest son of a retired army officer, was born at Broadstairs. His childhood, apart from prep school, was spent at the family home in Windsor Forest. At the age of thirteen he entered Winchester College, spending what were to be the happiest six years of his life there. Johnson referred to Winchester as the 'home of my heart'.[25] In his own family, with its military traditions, he was an anomaly – short, frail and introvert. John Francis Russell (later the second Earl) who knew Johnson at Winchester, described his parents as 'very narrow-minded and prejudiced Anglicans'.[26] Home, for Lionel, was 'Philistia'.[27]

It was, no doubt, Johnson's desire to create a more personal background for himself which led him to speculate on his lineage, in a varied if not contradictory manner. To one friend, in 1884, he claimed descent from a Scottish Border family – 'when we were a clan of the Johnstones'[28] – while to another, a year later, he declared, 'I belong by race in part to Guernsey, and look upon the Channel Islands as my home: though without living there.'[29] After visits to Dublin in 1893 and 1894 came the transformation of himself into an Irishman.

Johnson's career at Winchester was studded with honours. Two consecutive years he was author of the school prize poem, gaining prizes also for English Literature and English Essay. He edited *The Wykhamist* magazine; was a senior Prefect, Prefect of Chapel, and a member of the Mission Committee, and he also acted. Moreover, the correspondence he had as a precocious schoolboy between sixteen and eighteen with three young Oxford friends (J. F. Russell, J. H. Badley and Charles Sayle), shows the growth of a mind essentially subtle and sophisticated.

A selection of this correspondence edited by Russell appeared in 1919 under the title of *Some Winchester Letters of Lionel Johnson*, but was withdrawn from publication at the request of Johnson's relatives. The letters – whose staple ingredient is religious discussion – show his passage through some of the higher theisms (traditional or privately synthetic) to an *outward* acceptance of higher Anglicanism. The adjective here is advisedly stressed, since though

16

he can talk about the 'glorious festivals' of the Church and its 'ritualistic adorabilities', he can blithely envisage a possible need of filling the Church 'with Atheist priests if you like: with Arians, Unitarians, Anythingarians: but we must fill it.' For he had 'a very firm faith in hierarchy as a need of humanity', saying, 'I almost think true lives impossible without a kind of ceremonial creed.' In 'Nihilism', a poem written in 1889, occurs the significant statement: 'of life I am afraid.' Yet, to employ Newman's distinction, once he had reached a position of outward or 'nominal consent' to the Christian faith, he went on to act *as if* these assumptions were inwardly true, and by this type of pragmatism arrived at 'real consent'. In 1891 he was received into the Catholic Church.

Only a carefully edited portion of his correspondence appears in *Some Winchester Letters*, but it is not difficult to read between the lines a drama of antinomian feeling. 'In his last two years [at Winchester] Johnson was,' as Dr Iain Fletcher tells us, 'one of the leaders of a homosexual circle.'[30]

Johnson went up to Oxford in 1886. During his time at Oxford the Johnson legend of the poet as a learned, precious, noctambulistic figure, replete with a 'pontifical gravity'[31] of manner crystallized. It was Oxford too, as G. F. Russell observed, which 'saw the beginning of the tragedy which culminated in his early cutting off'[32] – a habit of largely secret drinking which was to increase till his death when he was consuming more than two pint bottles of whisky every twenty-four hours. Barbara Charlesworth comments how 'When Santayana first visited Johnson in the latter's room at Oxford, he noticed . . . a secular shrine on a centre table. A jug of Glengary whisky stood open between two open books: *Les Fleurs du Mal* and *Leaves of Grass*; looking down upon them were portraits of Cardinal Newman and Cardinal Wiseman.' She remarks that these arrangements had 'the quality of a still life', but that this was not nearly so important as 'the fact that the two books have an air of holiness, as if two Mass books were open at once upon an altar'.[33]

For the thirteen years to his death Johnson continued that habit of wide reading and study which hallmarked his years at school and university, but without developing any new attitudes. To the end, his prose was written with the care which distinguished his first essays and reviews. His verse diminished in quantity from about

1895. Dr Iain Fletcher tells us that there seems no doubt that Johnson's homosexual practices were 'discontinued after his reception into the Latin Church', and that the 'extravagant cult of friendship' which he substituted for such relationships proved 'a shadow without substance'.[34]

At Winchester and Oxford, he had elaborated a cult of lost causes, 'a sense of defeated aristocracy and a contempt . . . for the world around him'.[35] Membership of the Church of Rome anticipated in his Winchester letters and a dedication to Irish Nationalism in the mid-nineties merely added to this a feeling for 'martyrdoms that the world has forgotten'.[36]

He contributed many leading articles to *The Academy* and some half-dozen other papers and reviews. His book *The Art of Thomas Hardy* (1894) made his name as a critic, and the publication of his first volume of verse, *Poems* (1895), confirmed the high opinion of him as a poet formed on his pieces in *The Book of the Rhymers' Club* (1892) and *The Second Book of the Rhymers' Club* (1894) – the slim anthologies of that celebrated *cénacle* which had named Johnson, a foremost member of it, as its 'Receiver of Verse'.

But these were the years in which alcohol 'the servant had broken bounds for ever'.[37] Increasingly, his mode of life began to make a recluse of this 'sort of young old man'.[38] Yet as he declined, his cult of courtesy held public exposure at bay. William Rothenstein recalled, 'In person, he was scrupulously neat and his habits were quiet and studious. No one, not seeing him constantly, would have suspected his weakness.'[39] After partially overcoming an 'illness' which kept him confined to his rooms for over a year, he died in St Bartholomew's Hospital.

4 Lionel Johnson: Work

Lionel Johnson's work in verse is not an extensive body of writing: *Poems* (1895), *Ireland, with Other Poems* (1897) and a posthumous collection *The Complete Poems of Lionel Johnson* edited by Iain Fletcher (1953) which contains selected juvenilia and uncollected poems (1888–1902). Johnson's long first poem on Winchester, written in 1889 and dedicated to Campbell Dodgson, names in one stanza the main elements in his emotional existence – names them whether for good or ill:

> A place of friends! a place of books!
> A place of good things olden!
> With these delights, the years were golden;
> And life wore sunny looks.
> They fled at last:
> But to that past
> Am I in all beholden.

'Names them for ill' may sound a harsh comment upon so amiable a list of aspects; but the friends were often homosexual cronies, and the repression of this sexual passion, one or two years later, became his cross. As for the books and 'good things olden', they increasingly became a *modus vivendi* behind which he hid from 'reality'.

When he wrote this poem, Johnson was only twenty-two. Looking back on Winchester from Oxford, he sees his life there in terms of an interesting nostalgic vision, explainable by what Cyril Connolly has called 'The Theory of Permanent Adolescence', 'a theory that the experiences undergone by boys at the great public schools, their glories and disappointments, are so intense as to dominate their lives and arrest their development. From these it results that the greater part . . . remains adolescent, school-minded, self-conscious . . . sentimental and in the last analysis homosexual.'[40] This statement is clearly relevant to Johnson.

Veiled homosexual responsiveness was a leading incentive to his imagination. There is only one poem anywhere near explicit on the subject – the Latin verses to Oscar Wilde evidently composed upon receiving from him a copy of his novel *In Honorem Doriani Creatorisque Eius*, with its reference to 'apples of Sodom . . . hearts of vices; and sweet sins'.[41] The poem, attributed to 1890 or 1891, is a panegyric of Wilde, and was probably written about two months before Johnson was received into the Catholic Church. In the same year, he had introduced his friend Lord Alfred Douglas to Wilde; and the sonnet 'The Destroyer of a Soul' (1892), presumably addressed to Wilde, shows how Johnson had changed his tune.

For the most part though – at least on paper – he managed to transform his homosexual feelings into a cult of friendship. Almost every single poem in his two volumes of verse is dedicated to some individual. There are two poems by Johnson entitled 'A Friend', one of which ('His are the whitenesses of soul,/That Virgil had . . .') Paul Elmer More describes as sanctifying friendship 'almost as if it were a sacrament of the faith'.[42] This also applies to the other poem, so titled, dedicated to an actor, H. B. Irving (son of the famous Sir Henry):

> All, that he came to give,
> He gave, and went again:
> I have seen one man live,
> I have seen one man reign,
> With all the graces in his train.

Next to friendship, Johnson hymned Winchester as 'a place of books'; and his poetry is often bookish, as the following titles indicate: 'Oxford', 'Oxford Nights', 'The Classics', 'Plato in London', 'Virgil' and 'Walter Pater'. 'He worked at the creation of a self,' states Barbara Charlesworth, 'through identification with those who attracted him. He searched his library for fragments to shore against his ruin';[43] while Ezra Pound maintained that his poems might be considered as 'literary criticism in verse'.[44]

Johnson's liking for 'things olden' was more than a preference: it was a religion. Ezra Pound spoke of him as 'a traditionalist of traditionalists',[45] and Le Gallienne described him as 'a literary Catholic believing devoutly in the apostolic succession of all really great writers'.[46] Religiously and politically, this led him to espouse God and King Charles, the *ancien régime* and the old religion. Of *Poems* (1895), Le Gallienne wrote that 'we put down the volume firmly determined to join the Legitimist League tomorrow.'[47] Expressive of this aspect of Johnson are such poems as 'By the Statue of King Charles at Charing Cross', 'The Church of a Dream', 'The Age of a Dream' and 'Te Martyrum Candidatus'. In identifying himself with Irish nationalism, he thought of himself as defending an establishment far older than that established by Elizabeth's Protestant ascendancy. Then, too, by the middle of the nineties, he had come to believe himself an Irishman: 'Ireland,' writes Dr Iain Fletcher, 'was Johnson's last, most illusive dream.'[48]

Ireland, with Other Poems (1897) is commonly held to contain less good work than the first volume. Even Johnson himself may have had some doubts of it, though when he described it as 'hopelessly in the would-be austere and hieratic manner' he was locating an element also to be discovered in his first book. None the less, for Paul Elmer More, 'Ireland' was 'the one great . . . and genuinely significant poem of the present Gaelic movement'.

It was the masks assumed by Johnson, whether in prose or verse, which made him, in Imogen Guiney's words, 'a tower of wholesomeness in the decadence which his short life spanned'.[49] In his schoolboy letters he had described himself as 'an impressionist in life'; but later, as a literary critic, rebuked those disciples of 'the flowing philosophers' who sought to produce an adulterated literature of the senses. 'Symons,' he wrote of his fellow Rhymer in a letter to an inquiring friend, 'is a slave to impressionism, whether the impression be precious or not. A London fog, the blurred, tawny lamplight, the red omnibus, the dreary rain, the depressing mud, the glaring gin-shop, the slatternly shivering women: three dexterous stanzas, telling you that and nothing more.'[50]

These masks donned by Johnson represented his intellectual public faces. Another side is revealed in such poems as 'Mystic and Cavalier', 'The Dark Angel', 'Experience', 'Nihilism' and 'Vinum Dæmonum'. In his positive poems – his poetry of masks – Johnson was seeking to ignore or deny his tragedy. In the negative poems, he accepts it:

> The burden of the long gone years: the weight,
> The lifeless weight, of miserable things
> Done long ago, not done with: the live stings
> Left by old joys, follies provoking fate,
> Showing their sad side, when it is too late:
> Dread burden, that remorseless knowledge brings
> To men, remorseful! . . .

> ('Experience')

In the finest of these pieces, there is a gravity of utterance which deprives any self-corrosive thoughts of that sensationalism which might otherwise adhere to them. 'Vinum Dæmonum' treats of alcoholism, with an accounting statement of fatal appeal:

> Only one sting, and then but joy:
> One pang of fire, and thou art free.

> Then, what thou wilt, thou canst destroy:
> Save only me!

The best critical statements on Johnson's verse were made by Pound in his Preface to the 1915 edition of the poems. This Preface led to the book being withdrawn at the family's instigation, but it is reprinted in *The Literary Essays of Ezra Pound* (1954). His language is described as having 'an old-fashioned kind of precision', written in an English 'that has grown out of Latin'. Pound ventures an interesting comparison with Gautier, claiming that if that writer had not written, 'Johnson's work might even take its place in *Weltliteratur*, that it might stand for this clearness and neatness. In English literature it has some such place.'

5 John Davidson (1857–1909): Life

John Davidson was born at Barrhead, about six miles south of Glasgow, where his family moved in 1859. His father was a minister in the Evangelical Union. Like Arthur Symons, the child of a Methodist manse, Davidson rejected his religious patrimony but more extremely, becoming a militant atheist. A single term at Edinburgh University in 1876 provided him with ammunition against his father's limited opinions. As one of the characters in his *Fleet Street Eclogues*, clearly speaking for the poet, was to say:

> It was engraven deeply on my mind
> In daily lessons from my infancy
> Until I left my father's house, that not
> Ability and knowledge, beauty and strength,
> But goodness only can avail.

In adult life, he was to espouse a Nietzschean attitude of 'beyond good and evil', urging 'the generation knocking at the door', in his epigraph to *The Theatrocrat – A Tragic Play of Church and Stage* (1905), to

> Break – break it open; let the knocker rust:
> Consider no 'shalt not', and no man's 'must':
> And, being entered, promptly take the lead,
> Setting aside tradition, custom, creed . . .

Yet in daily living, he was very respectable, later expressing distaste for the bohemian ways of his younger colleagues in the Rhymers' Club.

Sent out to work at thirteen, Davidson later became a teacher. He combined his hated calling with writing, publishing a number of novels and verse-plays which carried a Scottish or northern imprint. Coming to London in 1890, he obtained review work from *The Academy*, *The Speaker* and *The Star*; and, through the good offices of Richard Le Gallienne, became one of the regarded authors of the Bodley Head. Soon he was telling Yeats that he was being paid forty pounds each for his ballads, while at the same time making his name as the journalists' bard with his *Fleet Street Eclogues*.

Inclined to take the current aestheticism as affectation, Davidson wrote concerning the production of his book that 'there was to be nothing fanciful for him – plain, honest, dark blue buckram was what he wanted.' This tendency to confuse the exquisite with the foppish was one of the causes of his difference with the other members of the Rhymers' Club; his exasperation with Herbert Horne, that greatly gifted amateur and editor of *The Hobby Horse* – 'If a man must be a connoisseur, let him be a connoisseur in women' – becoming a much-quoted dictum of the decade. Jealous of the enthusiastic response accorded to Dowson's 'Cynara' he remarked: 'I say this poem is not a fine poem, it is not even a good poem.' Somewhat more humorously, incensed at another contemporary 'puffed into popularity', he wrote:

> Because our Homer sometimes nods
>   The Ancient Bard who went before
> Is that a reason, oh ye Gods,
>   Should Stephen Phillips always snore.

In England, with its cult of polite moderation, Davidson remained a square peg in a round hole even as he had done in puritanical Scotland. When he came to London, he was already thirty-three, some ten years older than most of the young poets of the Rhymers' Club. Unlike some of these poets, he had a wife and children; but he lacked the academic qualifications or financial resources which others of them had. For six years, his books were issued by the Bodley Head, and afterwards by the young Grant Richards who, with the bankruptcy of Leonard Smithers in 1900, had taken over the publication of the aesthetic avant-garde. Already, by the middle of the nineties, he had spent the first force of his inspiration. 'The fires are out,' he had told Yeats, 'and I must hammer the cold iron.'[51]

For financial reasons he turned his hand to drama, but as for journalism, he declared himself unfitted 'for anything at all indeed except poetry: prose takes me more time and effort'.[52] In the last decade of his life, his biographer, J. Benjamin Townsend, remarks how 'the poet had sacrificed the fulfilment of his lyric powers to expound [in his five Testaments] a materialistic creed patched together from Darwin, Nietzsche and other revolutionary nine-teenth-century thinkers.'[53] Increasingly, he appeared 'very opiniona-ted, chronically angry with the world for not taking him at his own evaluation'.[54] Frank Harris thought of him as seeking to become 'the Blake of atheism'; and believed his pride was megalomaniacal. In 1907, he was granted a Civil List pension and moved down to Penzance for health reasons. Two years later he committed suicide. Over thirty years earlier, he had written to Swinburne saying that if he did not succeed 'by means of a pistol or laudanum I will regain that inheritance which you and I and all poets have lost'. William Watson wrote in *The Times* of 26 April 1909 that, 'John Davidson died because he could not make a living . . . his blood is upon us, as surely as if we had slain him with our own hands.'

6 John Davidson: Work

Compared with the work of the other Rhymers' Club poets, David-son's output is more substantial and original, but also more uneven. Leaving aside his books of drama and prose, Davidson's work is contained in fourteen volumes. *In a Music Hall* (1891) is apprentice work, not without touches of raciness and vigour. With *Fleet Street Eclogues* (1893) and a Second Series in 1896, he came into his own, creating a poetry in which imagery from the worlds of country and town met in a fresh attractive fashion. The diction of these poems also achieved a telling combination of Elizabethan rhetoric and contemporary colloquial speech.

Along with these two volumes of his prime, came a series of

titles which, even more, established him for half a decade: *Ballads and Songs* (1894), *New Ballads* (1897) and *The Last Ballad and Other Poems* (1899). These express, within effective narrative limits, his vision of humanity and his views on society, sex and art before the philosophic megalomania of his five *Testaments* had imprisoned and distorted his imagination. Appearing in *The Yellow Book*, his poem *The Ballad of a Nun* fluttered the late Victorian dovecots with blasphemy, eroticism and a message of free-love. Owen Seaman's splendid parody *A Ballad of a Bun*, while scoring a palpable hit or two, only served to advertise Davidson better. Less linguistically inventive, these poems possess the unity which the *Eclogues* lacked.

With the publication of *The Last Ballad and Other Poems*, the greater part of Davidson's work in lyric poetry was finished. From henceforth he concentrated on his didactic long poems: *The Testament of a Vivisector* (1901), *The Testament of a Man Forbid* (1901), *The Testament of an Empire Builder* (1902), *The Testament of a Prime Minister* (1904), and *The Testament of John Davidson* (1908). Of these works George Bernard Shaw remarked that they represented 'an attempt to raise modern materialism to the level of high poetry and eclipse Lucretius'.[55] But the poet's self-conceit and lack of self-criticism prevented all chances of success in this: 'I write for three people. Dante, Shakespeare and Jesus Christ,'[56] he once told Ernest Rhys! In fact, the latest writer on Davidson, Norman Alford, in his book *The Rhymers' Club*, regards him as being 'a more superficial intellect and emotionally off-balance' than his colleagues of the Rhymers' Club.

Davidson's three final plays *The Theatrocrat* (1905), *The Triumph of Mammon* (1907) *Mammon and His Message* (1908) are the dramatic counterpart of his misfiring *Testaments*. His early volume of *Plays* (1894), including the pastiche *Scaramouche in Naxos: A Pantomime*, was dubbed 'Shakespearean' on account of the fact that it contained much Elizabethanese, but the poet retorted that he had always been 'a Davidsonian'. Among various other books *The Wonderful Mission of Earl Lavender* (1895) is of interest as a skit on the *fin-de-siècle* spirit, though it lacks the sure touch of Robert Hitchens' *The Green Carnation*.

7 Dowson, Johnson, Davidson: A Comparison

All three of these poets were members of that loose *cénacle* of poets (a coterie or club without rules and officers) known as the Rhymers' Club which functioned between 1891 and 1894, exhibiting in the two anthologies it produced some of the finest poems of the decade. 'Twelve very competent verse writers'[57] is how the Rhymers have collectively been described and the phrase admirably defines most of its members. 'Dainty' and 'finicking' are terms that aptly describe the work of Victor Plarr, Herbert Horne, Ernest Rhys and others, but as well as W. B. Yeats, 'the central figure of the gathering',[58] Arthur Symons and the three poets included in this book belie this description. Such fellow Rhymers and associates as Plarr, Horne, Selwyn Image and G. A. Greene produced craftsmanlike verse which is sometimes exquisite, but they did not leave work stamped with its author's life-style. Though the verse of Dowson, Davidson and Johnson is not confessional in the almost literal and continuous manner of D. H. Lawrence's poetry, the quintessence of the poets' lives is interpretably present in their poems.

Yeats in his *Autobiographies* named his fellow Rhymers 'the tragic generation' and his father called them 'the Hamlets of our age'.[59] Both phrases were apt ones for that Gallicized group of young men who were the British equivalent of Verlaine's *poètes maudits*. It is the older man's *mot*, however, which gets to the heart of the affair, implying, as it does, that these writers were up against dilemmas in their nature which they were unable to resolve.

> You had to face your ends when young –
> 'Twas wine or women, or some curse –

wrote W. B. Yeats afterwards of these

> Poets with whom I learned my trade,
> Companions of the Cheshire Cheese.

Yet all that Dowson, Davidson and Johnson may be thought to share as poets was an attempt at 'writing lyrics technically perfect, their emotion pitched high'.[60] Even this is an over-generalization since Davidson's 'Thirty Bob a Week', though flawed by certain intellectual 'impurities', constitutes, along with Oscar Wilde's 'Reading Gaol', a rare example of the deeply impressive 'poem of some length' written in the nineties.

In a radio broadcast, T. S. Eliot once described Davidson as a poet 'who had genius but the incapacity for perfection', and this statement helps to explain Davidson's attitude to the other members of the Rhymers' Club. Morley Roberts, a friend of his, reported Davidson's own conviction that 'all of the Rhymers would not make one man of his worth.' Pathological as his self-opinion later grew to be, his sense of the difference between his own work and that of his Rhymer colleagues was based on sure intuition. He had, remarked Max Beerbohm, 'what I think the other poets had not: genius (and very robust genius)'; while another witness, Le Gallienne, adds his own critical evidence. 'There is', he wrote in 1894, 'a burliness of constitution underlying his most delicate fanciful work. . . . There is not another among them [the younger men] of whom it can be said . . . they suggest no such liberal strength as Mr. Davidson's least perfect work always suggests.'

This secret (sometimes vocal) sense of superiority over the other members of the Rhymers' Club was strengthened by Davidson's contempt for what he took to be the littleness of their aims. Yeats reports that, 'He saw in delicate, laborious, discriminating taste, an effeminate pedantry, and would, when the mood was on him, delight in all that seemed healthy, popular and bustling.'[61] With such feelings of separatist distinction, Davidson refused to contribute to the two anthologies of the Rhymers' Club or to become 'an out-and-out member . . . saying that he did not care to be ranked as one of a coterie.'[62]

There is no real artistic distance between the verse of Ernest Dowson and Lionel Johnson, say, as that between Davidson and his fellow members of the Rhymers' Club. T. Earle Welby stresses their similarities before concluding:

Far from being Celtic, Lionel Johnson has always seemed to me with Ernest Dowson among the most Latinate English poets of the latter part of the nineteenth century. . . .

Where Lionel Johnson and Dowson part company is where lyrical cadences become an inspiration. Lionel Johnson has a fine ear, but he is without spontaneity of rhythm. His music is made, with a scholar's care and to a noble scheme; never is it that trembling of the strings which enchants the reader of some of the best of Dowson's lyrics. He cares too much for the individual words to have Dowson's capacity for emulating Verlaine in what are sometimes almost literally *Romances sans Paroles*. And then, to go into the characters of the men so far as their work was affected by their lives, there is far more personal significance in most of Dowson's work than in all but one poem by Lionel Johnson. The exception is 'The Dark Angel', the poem into which he put his tragedy as completely as Dowson put his into 'Cynara'. The question will, however, suggest itself, which of the two tragedies more mattered to the victim?[63]

8 Their Influence

Davidson, the most imperfect of these three poets, had the most significant influence on the poetry which was to be written later. Although much of his work is flawed, he had a stronger imagination. But his impact lay not in the evolutionary materialism of his thought which he himself so much esteemed, but in its trappings: the colloquial note and urban imagery.

T. S. Eliot has recorded how, when he was a young tyro at Harvard, it was 'only the poets of the 'nineties . . . who at that period of history seemed to have anything to offer to me as a beginner', instancing three of them by name: Symons, Dowson and Davidson. 'I got the idea,' he continued, 'that one could write poetry in an English such as one would speak oneself. A colloquial idiom. There was a spoken rhythm in some of their poems.'[64] Earlier, in a broadcast, he had paid specific respect to Davidson's 'Thirty Bob a Week' ('his one great achievement . . . I know nothing quite like it'). Published in *Ballads and Songs* (1894), it may be thought of as giving a civilian voice to the military vernacular of Kipling's *Barrack Room Ballads* which had appeared two years earlier.

Nevertheless, this achieved colloquial note is to be found in Davidson only occasionally. His ballads feature much writing in dialogue and monologue; but, for the most part, employ the histrionic rhetoric of Elizabethan and Jacobean drama, as in 'A Ballad of a Workman' and 'A Ballad in Blank Verse'. Only one other poem

28

by him experiments in an interesting manner with the colloquial, namely 'Rail and Raid' – an otherwise largely unsuccessful piece appearing in his posthumous volume *Fleet Street and Other Poems* (1909) – whose middle passage seeks to convey the interminable chatter of a railway-compartment bore.

Too little attention has been accorded Davidson's other contribution to twentieth-century poetry – his metropolitan imagery. In his Preface to the edition of Davidson just quoted, Eliot confessed that, like the nineties poets, 'he had a good many dingy urban images to reveal', those not assuming the dress of Laforgue being nearer in manner to those of Symons (with their hinting at a Prufrockian bohemia) than to those of Davidson. Of the Rhymers themselves – Davidson excepted – it was Symons chiefly who had elaborated the metropolitan cartography in his poems. But Symons' London was largely a townscape of selected corners, choice spots and romantic vistas or prospects, for the most part imbued with a special atmosphere – Temple, the Embankment, Kensington Gardens, etc. It was also a somewhat demi-mondain terrain where the women were actresses, ballet-girls or whores, and where the men did not exist at all.

Davidson does not only describe certain representative men and women who make up the vast megapolis, but enters imaginatively into the pattern of their lives and fates (the poor clerk in 'Thirty Bob a Week', and the tramps, scavengers and kerb-sellers in 'Liverpool Street'). In 'Holiday at Hampton Court' (from *The Last Ballad and Other Poems*, 1899) he paints the crowd in its Bank Holiday recreation, returning to the subject a decade later in 'The Crystal Palace' (from *Fleet Street and Other Poems*, 1909), the second attempt being verbally less finished but more realistic in incident and diction.

He also pushes back the boundaries of London on the poetic map in order to take in the house-and-garden suburbs and the pastoral fringes. 'November' (from *Holiday and Other Poems*, 1906) offers us a sequence of six vignettes: Regent's Park, the Enfield Road, Epping Forest, Box Hill, London, W., and the Chilterns. Living at Hornsey, as he did when he first came to London, Davidson would often take a north-bound direction when seeking release from the built-up area; 'A Northern Suburb' records the town's continued encroachment on the land:

> In gaudy yellow brick and red,
>> With rooting pipes, like creepers rank,
> The shoddy terraces o'erspread
>> Meadow, and garth, and daisied bank.

> With shelves for rooms the houses crowd,
>> Like draughty cupboards in a row –
> Ice-chests when wintry winds are loud,
>> Ovens when summer breezes blow.

The advent of our new towns since the war only makes this poem more socially valid. One might hazard a guess – to instance but two names – that Edgell Rickword and Sir John Betjeman have read and digested such poems as this.

With the exception of the ungainly *Testaments*, it is, oddly, Davidson's later poems which are most 'modernist' in subject and diction while being, at the same time, most technically and formally unfinished. Besides the pieces already cited in *Fleet Street and Other Poems* (1909), there are others which enshrine brief vignettes of the contemporary scene – swiftly passing images of *things clearly seen* – surrounded by a welter of verbose writing. 'The Thames Embankment' and the title poem particularly repay study. Yet it cannot be claimed that Davidson wrote a single *entire* poem in the 'modern' idiom; the nearest he came to it being 'In the Isle of Dogs' from his last volume of verse published in the nineties, *The Last Ballad and Other Poems*. Its first twenty-four lines mix contemporaneity of reference with a fairly sparse diction; but from then on till its end some forty lines later, a literary-romantic language takes over.

Dowson's influence on posterity was two-fold: first, and more influential, a cult of passion, languor and despair, expressed not so much in any distinctive technique as present, generally, in a mood or a theme; and, secondly, a vogue for 'la musique avant toutes choses' – speech approximating as closely as possible to music – an aspect of 'pure poetry', of which Edith Sitwell's early pieces are attractive and amusing examples.

The former element is present in the work of Edmund John (1883–1917), a forgotten poet of the nineties aftermath who published two volumes of verse, *Flute of Sardonyx* (1913) and *Symphonie Symbolique* (1919). More manifestly, it can be recognized in Richard Middleton's posthumous *Poems and Songs* (First and Second Series) published in 1912.

> Now, in this sombre and regretful place,
>   Grey when the sun has crimsoned all the west,
> With sorrow like a mask upon my face,
>   I lay my dreams to rest.

This is from 'In Memoriam'; while numerous poems with ladies' names as titles – Christine, Irene, Dorothy, Lilian – vamp upon the burden of Dowson's 'Cynara'.

Aldous Huxley, in one of the prose poems in his book *Leda* (1920), mocked at this cult of passion and despair:

'Sans Espoir, sans Espoir . . .' sang the lady while the piano laboriously opened its box of old sardines in treacle. One detected ptomaine in the syrup.

Sans Espoir . . . I thought of the rhymes – soir, nonchaloir, reposoir – the dying falls of a symbolism grown sadly suicidal before the broad Flemish back of the singer, the dewlaps of her audience. Sans Espoir. The listeners wore the frozen rapture of those who gaze upon the uplifted Host.

But the laughter, as so frequently with Huxley, was an aspect of temperamental fascination. Earlier he had contributed an essay on Dowson to the fifth volume of Ward's *English Poets* ('His poetry is the poetry of resignation, not of rebellion. He suffers and records the fact. That is enough . . .'), and in the poem 'Carpe Noctem' published as late as 1931, he had echoed that combination of hedonism and pessimism so classically declared by Dowson:

> There is no future, there is no more past,
> No roots nor fruits, but momentary flowers.
> Lie still, only lie still and night will last,
> Silent and dark, not for a space of hours,
> But everlastingly. Let me forget
> All but your perfume, every night but this,
> The shame, the fruitless weeping, the regret.[65]

From the time of 'Laurence Hope' (Adela Florence Nicolson) to John Gawsworth, the feeling-tone of Dowson's poems has been well reproduced in English verse, 'Pale hands I loved beside the Shali-mar'[66] being a sort of popularization of Dowson's more esoteric passion.

As Eliot remarked of Milton, Dowson was a poet who worked mainly through 'the auditory imagination'. The four translations from Verlaine contained in *Decorations* (1899) came as near to distilling the spirit of those *Romances sans Paroles* as any English-man, with the possible exception of Symons, had done. The same economy of diction is found in many of Dowson's own pieces, leading Rupert Brooke in 1906, during his last term at Rugby, to speak with approval of Dowson's verse as coming 'as near to faint music as speech can come'. In practice, Brooke never achieved this effect of Dowson, his own preference inclining him to the Elizabethan sonnets rather than to the lyrics and songs of that period and later. The closest approximation of any later poet to the Dowson of, say, 'A Requiem', 'Beata Solitudo' or 'A Valediction' is Richard Middle-ton with a handful of poems. These too often – as with 'Lullaby' or 'The Flower-Girl' – are flawed with obviousness or sentimentality; but there are others which offer, if only for a stanza or two at a time, something of Dowson's rare felicity:

> The girls are flushed with wine,
> And singing in the shade,
> And wanton words invade
> Their delicate mouths that pine
> Through kissing of the vine,
> And every golden maid
> Loves, though she be betrayed,
> The stars, the stars that shine.

('The Happy Cruise')

Johnson, a learned reactionary, consciously harked back to the past, and has been the least influential of the trio. Nevertheless, Ezra Pound showed interest in him, noting in his Preface to the *Poetical Works of Lionel Johnson* (1915) that though much of John-son's verse was written in 'a bookish dialect . . . a curial speech', its language possessed 'an old-fashioned kind of precision'.

This admission was indirect praise from one who in 1912 had

decided with H.D. and Richard Aldington that two of the principles of their school should be 'Direct treatment of the "thing" whether subjective or objective' and 'To use absolutely no word that does not contribute to the presentation.' How sparse and pared are both diction and rhythm in 'Parnell', written in 1893:

> The wail of Irish winds,
> The cry of Irish seas:
> Eternal sorrow finds
> Eternal voice in these.
>
> I cannot praise our dead,
> Whom Ireland weeps so well:
> Her morning light, that fled;
> Her morning star, that fell.

Johnson is not eminently a poet with a visual imagination, but of his line 'Blue lie the fields and fade into the sky' Pound notes that 'it has a beauty like the Chinese'. This was written in the same year as he published *Cathay*. As Eliot observed of Pound's work to 1928, 'the shades of Dowson, Lionel Johnson and Fiona [Macleod] flit about.'

'Poets said to one over their black coffee,' recalled Yeats some forty years later, ' "we must purify poetry of all that is not poetry," and by poetry they meant poetry as it had been written by Catullus, a great name at that time, by the Jacobean writers, by Verlaine, by Baudelaire.'[67] Maurice Lindsay brightly applied the epithet 'tutti frutti' to the Victorian verse against which the men of the Rhymers reacted. This compositional *mélange* was held by the Rhymers to represent a corruption of poetry. Poems as full of moral sermonizing as certain of Tennyson's, or political eloquence as some of Swinburne's, or psychological curiosity so prevalent in Browning's appeared to them as adulterated creations. In their own way, they were working towards a poetic counterpart of that theory of Significant Form which Clive Bell and Roger Fry first adumbrated some time before 1913.

Dowson's poetry certainly answers to this memorable formal patterning of emotion which one may take to be the essence of the theory. Much of Johnson's poetry, and a good percentage of Davidson's likewise, can be embraced by this formula. In Dowson, purposive ethical content is nil. In Johnson and Davidson, it does sometimes occur, but fused with the other ingredients of the poem by means of a subjective or aesthetic emotion; only Davidson's last work reverts to the old didacticism. In their poetics of what is aesthetically quintessential, these three poets are a bridge between Victorianism and the twentieth century as represented by the trad-modernism of Eliot, Pound and the mature Yeats. There is, for example, plenty of passionate moral contemplation in the latter's later work, but such a poem as 'Easter 1916', say, would not have been written by him had he not learned his trade with those 'Companions of the Cheshire Cheese'.

A Note on the Text

The texts which I have employed in the case of the first two poets are those of Sir Desmond Flower's *The Poetical Works of Ernest Dowson* (3rd ed, 1967) and Dr Iain Fletcher's *The Complete Poems of Lionel Johnson* (1953), to whose publishers Messrs Cassell and the Unicorn Press I make my grateful acknowledgements. To the editors themselves I must make known my deepest respect and debt, since they have been foremost in pioneering a knowledge of these poets in a perspective of the nineties. With the third poet I have whenever possible used the text of Maurice Lindsay's *John Davidson: A Selection of His Poems* (1961). To Mr Lindsay and his publishers Messrs Hutchinson grateful acknowledgements are due. When the poem chosen was not included here, I worked from the early editions of John Lane and Grant Richards. (Andrew Turnbull's standard edition, *The Poems of John Davidson* (2 vols., 1973) appeared when this selection was going to press.)

Notes

(Place of publication in all cases is London, unless otherwise stated.)

1 Quoted from Conal O'Riordan in *The Letters of Ernest Dowson*, ed. Desmond Flower and Henry Maas, 1967.

2 Victor Plarr, *Ernest Dowson*, 1914.
3 W. R. Thomas, 'Ernest Dowson at Oxford', *The Nineteenth Century*, April 1928.
4 Arthur Symons, *The Savoy*, August 1896.
5 Thomas, in *The Nineteenth Century*, April 1928.
6 Edgar Jepson, *Memoirs of a Victorian*, 1933.
7 *The Letters of Ernest Dowson*, ed. Flower and Maas.
8 Ibid.
9 Ibid.
10 Ibid.
11 Jepson, *Memoirs of a Victorian*.
12 Plarr, *Dowson*.
13 Robert Harborough Sherard, *Bernard Shaw, Frank Harris & Oscar Wilde*, 1937.
14 Gertrude Atherton, *Adventures of a Novelist*, 1932.
15 *The Poetical Works of Ernest Dowson*, ed. Desmond Flower, 1967.
16 *The Poetical Works of Ernest Dowson*, 1967.
17 *The Letters of Ernest Dowson*, 1967.
18 Ibid.
19 Ibid.
20 John Gawsworth, 'The Dowson Legend', in *Essays by Divers Hands*, New series, xvii (1938).
21 B. Ifor Evans, *English Poetry in the Later Nineteenth Century*, 1933.
22 Frank Harris, *Contemporary Portraits*, 2nd series, 1919.
23 Ibid.
24 Arthur Symons, 'Ernest Dowson', in *Studies in Prose and Verse*, 1904.
25 *Some Winchester Letters of Lionel Johnson*, ed. J. F. Russell, 1919.
26 Ibid.
27 Ibid.
28 Ibid.
29 Ibid.
30 *The Complete Poems of Lionel Johnson*, ed. Iain Fletcher, 1953.
31 George Santayana, *The Middle Span*, 1947.
32 *Some Winchester Letters of Lionel Johnson*.
33 Barbara Charlesworth, *Dark Passages: The Decadent Consciousness in Victorian Literature*, Madison & Milwaukee, 1965.
34 *The Complete Poems of Lionel Johnson*, 1953.
35 Charlesworth, *Dark Passages*.
36 W. B. Yeats in *A Treasury of Irish Poetry in the English Tongue*, ed. S. A. Brooke and T. W. Rolleston, 1900.
37 *The Complete Poems of Lionel Johnson*, 1953.

38 Harris, *Contemporary Portraits*.
39 William Rothenstein, *Men and Memories 1872–1900*, 1931.
40 Cyril Connolly, *Enemies of Promise*, 1938.
41 Translated by Iain Fletcher in *The Complete Poems of Lionel Johnson*, 1953.
42 Paul Elmer More, 'Two Poets of the Irish Movement', in *Shelburne Essays*, First series, 1904.
43 Charlesworth, *Dark Passages*.
44 *Poetical Works of Lionel Johnson*, ed. Ezra Pound, 1915.
45 Ibid.
46 Richard Le Gallienne, 'Lionel Johnson's "Poems" ', *Retrospective Reviews*, II (1896).
47 Ibid.
48 *The Complete Poems of Lionel Johnson*, 1953.
49 Imogen Guiney, Obituary, *The Month*, Oct. 1902.
50 *Poetical Works of Lionel Johnson*, 1915.
51 W. B. Yeats, 'The Tragic Generation', in *The Trembling of the Veil*, 1922.
52 J. Benjamin Townsend, *John Davidson: Poet of Armageddon*, New Haven, 1961.
53 Ibid.
54 C. Lewis Hind, 'John Davidson', in *More Authors and I*, 1927.
55 Grant Richards, *Author Hunting*, 1934.
56 Quoted by Townsend in *John Davidson: Poet of Armageddon*.
57 Patricio Gannon, *Poets of the Rhymers' Club*, Buenos Aires, 1953.
58 Jepson, *Memoirs of a Victorian*.
59 *The Oxford Book of Modern Verse 1892–1935*, ed. W. B. Yeats, 1936.
60 Ibid.
61 W. B. Yeats, 'The Tragic Generation', in *The Trembling of the Veil*.
62 Ernest Rhys, *Everyman Remembers*, 1933.
63 T. Earle Welby, *Second Impressions*, 1933.
64 *John Davidson: A Selection of His Poems*, ed. Maurice Lindsay, 1961.
65 Aldous Huxley, *The Cicadas and Other Poems*, 1931.
66 Laurence Hope, 'Kashmiri Song', in *The Garden of Kama*, 1901.
67 *The Oxford Book of Modern Verse 1892–1935*.

Further Reading

Norman Alford, *The Rhymers' Club*, 1974.
Hayim Fineman, *John Davidson, a Study of the Relation of His Ideas to His Poetry*, 1916.

Desmond Flower and Henry Maas (eds.), *The Letters of Ernest Dowson*, 1967.

Mark Longaker, *Ernest Dowson*, 3rd ed., 1967.

Mark Longaker (ed.), *The Stories of Ernest Dowson*, 1949.

R. D. Macloud, *Poems and Ballads by John Davidson*, 1954.

Arthur W. Patrick, *Lionel Johnson, poète et critique*, Paris, 1939.

Derek Stanford, *Poets of the Nineties*, 1965.

Derek Stanford, *Writing of the Nineties*, 1971.

A. J. A. Symons, *An Anthology of 'Nineties Verse*, 1928.

R. K. R. Thornton, *Poetry of the 'Nineties*, 1970.

Priscilla Thoules, *Modern Poetic Drama*, 1934, (one chapter relevant to Davidson).

J. B. Townsend, *John Davidson: Poet of Armageddon*, New Haven, 1961.

Andrew Turnbull, *The Poems of John Davidson*, 1973.

Ernest Dowson

From *Verses*

Vitae summa brevis spem nos vetat incohare longam.

They are not long, the weeping and the laughter,
    Love and desire and hate:
I think they have no portion in us after
    We pass the gate.

They are not long, the days of wine and roses:
    Out of a misty dream
Our path emerges for a while, then closes
    Within a dream.

A Coronal

With His songs and Her days to His Lady
and to Love

Violets and leaves of vine,
    Into a frail, fair wreath
We gather and entwine:
    A wreath for Love to wear,
    Fragrant as his own breath,
To crown his brow divine,
    All day till night is near.
Violets and leaves of vine
We gather and entwine.

Violets and leaves of vine
  For Love that lives a day,
We gather and entwine.
  All day till Love is dead,
  Till eve falls, cold and gray,
These blossoms, yours and mine,
  Love wears upon his head.
Violets and leaves of vine
We gather and entwine.

Violets and leaves of vine,
  For Love when poor Love dies
We gather and entwine.
  This wreath that lives a day
  Over his pale, cold eyes,
Kissed shut by Proserpine,
  At set of sun we lay:
Violets and leaves of vine
We gather and entwine.

Nuns of the Perpetual Adoration

For the Countess Sobieska von Platt

Calm, sad, secure; behind high convent walls,
  These watch the sacred lamp, these watch and pray:
And it is one with them when evening falls,
  And one with them the cold return of day.

These heed not time; their nights and days they make
  Into a long, returning rosary,
Whereon their lives are threaded for Christ's sake:
  Meekness and vigilance and chastity.

A vowed patrol, in silent companies,
  Life-long they keep before the living Christ:
In the dim church, their prayers and penances
  Are fragrant incense to the Sacrificed.

Outside, the world is wild and passionate;
  Man's weary laughter and his sick despair
Entreat at their impenetrable gate:
  They heed no voices in their dream of prayer.

They saw the glory of the world displayed;
  They saw the bitter of it, and the sweet;
They knew the roses of the world should fade,
  And be trod under by the hurrying feet.

Therefore they rather put away desire,
  And crossed their hands and came to sanctuary;
And veiled their heads and put on coarse attire:
  Because their comeliness was vanity.

And there they rest; they have serene insight
  Of the illuminating dawn to be:
Mary's sweet Star dispels for them the night,
  The proper darkness of humanity.

Calm, sad, secure; with faces worn and mild:
  Surely their choice of vigil is the best?
Yea! for our roses fade, the world is wild;
  But there, beside the altar, there, is rest.

Villanelle of Sunset

  Come hither, Child! and rest:
    This is the end of day,
  Behold the weary West!

  Sleep rounds with equal zest
    Man's toil and children's play:
  Come hither, Child! and rest.

  My white bird, seek thy nest,
    Thy drooping head down lay:
  Behold the weary West!

Now are the flowers confest
  Of slumber: sleep, as they!
Come hither, Child! and rest.

Now eve is manifest,
  And homeward lies our way:
Behold the weary West!

Tired flower! upon my breast,
  I would wear thee alway:
Come hither, Child! and rest;
Behold, the weary West!

My Lady April

For Léopold Nelken

Dew on her robe and on her tangled hair;
Twin dewdrops for her eyes; behold her pass,
With dainty step brushing the young, green grass,
The while she trills some high, fantastic air,
Full of all feathered sweetness: she is fair,
And all her flower-like beauty, as a glass,
Mirrors out hope and love: and still, alas!
Traces of tears her languid lashes wear.
Say, doth she weep for very wantonness?
Or is it that she dimly doth foresee
Across her youth the joys grow less and less,
The burden of the days that are to be:
Autumn and withered leaves and vanity,
And winter bringing end in barrenness.

To One in Bedlam

For Henry Davray

With delicate, mad hands, behind his sordid bars,
Surely he hath his posies, which they tear and twine;
Those scentless wisps of straw, that miserably line
His strait, caged universe, whereat the dull world stares,

Pedant and pitiful. O, how his rapt gaze wars
With their stupidity! Know they what dreams divine
Lift his long, laughing reveries like enchanted wine,
And make his melancholy germane to the stars?

O lamentable brother! if those pity thee,
Am I not fain of all thy lone eyes promise me;
Half a fool's kingdom, far from men who sow and reap,
All their days, vanity? Better than mortal flowers,
Thy moon-kissed roses seem: better than love or sleep,
The star-crowned solitude of thine oblivious hours!

Ad Domnulam Suam

Little lady of my heart!
    Just a little longer,
Love me: we will pass and part,
    Ere this love grow stronger.

I have loved thee, Child! too well,
    To do aught but leave thee:
Nay! my lips should never tell
    Any tale, to grieve thee.

Little lady of my heart!
    Just a little longer,
I may love thee: we will part,
    Ere my love grow stronger.

Soon thou leavest fairy-land;
  Darker grow thy tresses:
Soon no more of hand in hand;
  Soon no more caresses!

Little lady of my heart!
  Just a little longer,
Be a child: then, we will part,
  Ere this love grow stronger.

Amor Umbratilis

A gift of Silence, sweet!
  Who may not ever hear:
To lay down at your unobservant feet,
  Is all the gift I bear.

I have no songs to sing,
  That you should heed or know:
I have no lilies, in full hands, to fling
  Across the path you go.

I cast my flowers away,
  Blossoms unmeet for you!
The garland I have gathered in my day:
  My rosemary and rue.

I watch you pass and pass,
  Serene and cold: I lay
My lips upon your trodden, daisied grass,
  And turn my life away.

Yea, for I cast you, sweet!
  This one gift, you shall take:
Like ointment, on your unobservant feet,
  My silence, for your sake.

Amor Profanus

For Gabriel de Lautrec

Beyond the pale of memory,
In some mysterious dusky grove;
A place of shadows utterly,
Where never coos the turtle-dove,
A world forgotten of the sun:
I dreamed we met when day was done,
And marvelled at our ancient love.

Met there by chance, long kept apart,
We wandered, through the darkling glades;
And that old language of the heart
We sought to speak: alas! poor shades!
Over our pallid lips had run
The waters of oblivion,
Which crown all loves of men or maids.

In vain we stammered: from afar
Our old desire shone cold and dead:
That time was distant as a star,
When eyes were bright and lips were red.
And still we went with downcast eye
And no delight in being nigh,
Poor shadows most uncomforted.

Ah, Lalage! while life is ours,
Hoard not thy beauty rose and white,
But pluck the pretty, fleeting flowers
That deck our little path of light:
For all too soon we twain shall tread
The bitter pastures of the dead:
Estranged, sad spectres of the night.

Villanelle of Marguerites

For Miss Eugénie Magnus

'A little, passionately, not at all?'
She casts the snowy petals on the air:
And what care we how many petals fall!

Nay, wherefore seek the seasons to forestall?
It is but playing, and she will not care,
A little, passionately, not at all!

She would not answer us if we should call
Across the years: her visions are too fair;
And what care we how many petals fall!

She knows us not, nor recks if she enthrall
With voice and eyes and fashion of her hair,
A little, passionately, not at all!

Knee-deep she goes in meadow grasses tall,
Kissed by the daisies that her fingers tear:
And what care we how many petals fall!

We pass and go: but she shall not recall
What men we were, nor all she made us bear:
'A little, passionately, not at all!'
And what care we how many petals fall!

Yvonne of Brittany

For Marmaduke Langdale

In your mother's apple-orchard,
   Just a year ago, last spring:
Do you remember, Yvonne!
   The dear trees lavishing
Rain of their starry blossoms
   To make you a coronet?
Do you ever remember, Yvonne?
   As I remember yet.

In your mother's apple-orchard,
   When the world was left behind:
You were shy, so shy, Yvonne!
   But your eyes were calm and kind.
We spoke of the apple harvest,
   When the cider press is set,
And such-like trifles, Yvonne!
   That doubtless you forget.

In the still, soft Breton twilight,
   We were silent; words were few,
Till your mother came out chiding,
   For the grass was bright with dew:
But I know your heart was beating,
   Like a fluttered, frightened dove.
Do you ever remember, Yvonne?
   That first faint flush of love?

In the fulness of midsummer,
   When the apple-bloom was shed,
Oh, brave was your surrender,
   Though shy the words you said.
I was glad, so glad, Yvonne!
   To have led you home at last;
Do you ever remember, Yvonne!
   How swiftly the days passed?

In your mother's apple-orchard
 It is grown too dark to stray,
There is none to chide you, Yvonne!
 You are over far away.
There is dew on your grave grass, Yvonne!
 But your feet it shall not wet:
No, you never remember, Yvonne!
 And I shall soon forget.

Benedictio Domini

For Selwyn Image

Without, the sullen noises of the street!
 The voice of London, inarticulate,
Hoarse and blaspheming, surges in to meet
 The silent blessing of the Immaculate.

Dark is the church, and dim the worshippers,
 Hushed with bowed heads as though by some old spell,
While through the incense-laden air there stirs
 The admonition of a silver bell.

Dark is the church, save where the altar stands,
 Dressed like a bride, illustrious with light,
Where one old priest exalts with tremulous hands
 The one true solace of man's fallen plight.

Strange silence here: without, the sounding street
 Heralds the world's swift passage to the fire:
O Benediction, perfect and complete!
 When shall men cease to suffer and desire?

Ad Manus Puellae

For Leonard Smithers

I was always a lover of ladies' hands!
　Or ever mine heart came here to tryst,
For the sake of your carved white hands' commands;
　The tapering fingers, the dainty wrist;
　The hands of a girl were what I kissed.

I remember an hand like a *fleur-de-lys*
　When it slid from its silken sheath, her glove;
With its odours passing ambergris:
　And that was the empty husk of a love.
　Oh, how shall I kiss your hands enough?

They are pale with the pallor of ivories;
　But they blush to the tips like a curled sea-shell:
What treasure, in kingly treasuries,
　Of gold, and spice for the thurible,
　Is sweet as her hands to hoard and tell?

I know not the way from your finger-tips,
　Nor how I shall gain the higher lands,
The citadel of your sacred lips:
　I am captive still of my pleasant bands,
　The hands of a girl, and most your hands.

Flos Lunae

For Yvanhoé Rambosson

I would not alter thy cold eyes,
Nor trouble the calm fount of speech
With aught of passion or surprise.
The heart of thee I cannot reach:
I would not alter thy cold eyes!

I would not alter thy cold eyes;
Nor have thee smile, nor make thee weep:
Though all my life droops down and dies,
Desiring thee, desiring sleep,
I would not alter thy cold eyes.

I would not alter thy cold eyes;
I would not change thee if I might,
To whom my prayers for incense rise,
Daughter of dreams! my moon of night!
I would not alter thy cold eyes.

I would not alter thy cold eyes,
With trouble of the human heart:
Within their glance my spirit lies,
A frozen thing, alone, apart;
I would not alter thy cold eyes.

Non Sum Qualis Eram Bonae
Sub Regno Cynarae

Last night, ah, yesternight, betwixt her lips and mine
There fell thy shadow, Cynara! thy breath was shed
Upon my soul between the kisses and wine;
And I was desolate and sick of an old passion,
    Yea, I was desolate and bowed my head:
I have been faithful to thee, Cynara! in my fashion.

All night upon mine heart I felt her warm heart beat,
Night-long within mine arms in love and sleep she lay;
Surely the kisses of her bought red mouth were sweet;
But I was desolate and sick of an old passion,
    When I awoke and found the dawn was gray:
I have been faithful to thee, Cynara! in my fashion.

I have forgot much, Cynara! gone with the wind,
Flung roses, roses riotously with the throng,
Dancing, to put thy pale, lost lilies out of mind;
But I was desolate and sick of an old passion,
　　Yea, all the time, because the dance was long:
I have been faithful to thee, Cynara! in my fashion.

I cried for madder music and for stronger wine,
But when the feast is finished and the lamps expire,
Then falls thy shadow, Cynara! the night is thine;
And I am desolate and sick of an old passion,
　　Yea hungry for the lips of my desire:
I have been faithful to thee, Cynara! in my fashion.

Vanitas

For Vincent O'Sullivan

Beyond the need of weeping,
　　Beyond the reach of hands,
May she be quietly sleeping,
　　In what dim nebulous lands?
Ah, she who understands!

The long, long winter weather,
　　These many years and days,
Since she, and Death, together,
　　Left me the wearier ways:
And now, these tardy bays!

The crown and victor's token:
　　How are they worth today?
The one word left unspoken,
　　It were late now to say:
But cast the palm away!

For once, ah once, to meet her,
    Drop laurel from tired hands:
Her cypress were the sweeter,
    In her oblivious lands:
Haply she understands!

Spleen

For Arthur Symons

I was not sorrowful, I could not weep,
And all my memories were put to sleep.

I watched the river grow more white and strange,
All day till evening I watched it change.

All day till evening I watched the rain
Beat wearily upon the window pane.

I was not sorrowful, but only tired
Of everything that ever I desired.

Her lips, her eyes, all day became to me
The shadow of a shadow utterly.

All day mine hunger for her heart became
Oblivion, until the evening came,

And left me sorrowful, inclined to weep,
With all my memories that could not sleep.

O Mors! Quam Amara est
Memoria Tua Homini Pacem
Habenti in Substantiis Suis

Exceeding sorrow
    Consumeth my sad heart!
Because tomorrow
    We must depart,
Now is exceeding sorrow
    All my part!

Give over playing,
    Cast thy viol away:
Merely laying
    Thine head my way:
Prithee, give over playing,
    Grave or gay.

Be no word spoken;
    Weep nothing: let a pale
Silence, unbroken
    Silence prevail!
Prithee, be no word spoken,
    Lest I fail!

Forget tomorrow!
    Weep nothing: only lay
In silent sorrow
    Thine head my way:
Let us forget tomorrow,
    This one day!

'You would have understood me, had you waited'

Ah, dans ces mornes séjours
Les jamais sont les toujours.
PAUL VERLAINE

You would have understood me, had you waited;
   I could have loved you, dear! as well as he:
Had we not been impatient, dear! and fated
      Always to disagree.

What is the use of speech? Silence were fitter:
   Lest we should still be wishing things unsaid.
Though all the words we ever spake were bitter,
      Shall I reproach you dead?

Nay, let this earth, your portion, likewise cover
   All the old anger, setting us apart:
Always, in all, in truth was I your lover;
      Always, I held your heart.

I have met other women who were tender,
   As you were cold, dear! with a grace as rare.
Think you, I turned to them, or made surrender,
      I who had found you fair?

Had we been patient, dear! ah, had you waited,
   I had fought death for you, better than he:
But from the very first, dear! we were fated
      Always to disagree.

Vain Resolves

I said: 'There is an end of my desire:
   Now have I sown, and I have harvested,
And these are ashes of an ancient fire,
   Which, verily, shall not be quickened.
Now will I take me to a place of peace,
    Forget mine heart's desire;
In solitude and prayer, work out my soul's release.

'I shall forget her eyes, how cold they were;
   Forget her voice, how soft it was and low,
With all my singing that she did not hear,
   And all my service that she did not know.
I shall not hold the merest memory
    Of any days that were,
Within those solitudes where I will fasten me.'

And once she passed, and once she raised her eyes,
   And smiled for courtesy, and nothing said:
And suddenly the old flame did uprise,
   And all my dead desire was quickened.
Yea! as it hath been, it shall ever be,
    Most passionless, pure eyes!
Which never shall grow soft, nor change, nor pity me.

A Requiem

For John Gray

   Neobule, being tired,
   Far too tired to laugh or weep,
   From the hours, rosy and gray,
   Hid her golden face away,
   Neobule, fain of sleep,
   Slept at last as she desired!

Neobule! is it well,
That you haunt the hollow lands,
Where the poor, dead people stray,
Ghostly, pitiful and gray,
Plucking, with their spectral hands,
Scentless blooms of asphodel?

Neobule, tired to death
Of the flowers that I threw
On her flower-like, fair feet,
Sighed for blossoms not so sweet,
Lunar roses pale and blue,
Lilies of the world beneath.

Neobule! ah, too tired
Of the dreams and days above!
Where the poor, dead people stray,
Ghostly, pitiful and gray,
Out of life and out of love,
Sleeps the sleep which she desired.

Beata Solitudo

For Sam. Smith

What land of Silence,
    Where pale stars shine
On apple-blossom
    And dew-drenched vine,
    Is yours and mine?

The silent valley
    That we will find,
Where all the voices
    Of humankind
    Are left behind.

There all forgetting,
    Forgotten quite,
We will repose us,
    With our delight
    Hid out of sight.

The world forsaken
    And out of mind
Honour and labour,
    We shall not find
    The stars unkind.

And men shall travail,
    And laugh and weep;
But we have vistas
    Of gods asleep,
    With dreams as deep.

A land of Silence,
    Where pale stars shine
On apple-blossoms
    And dew-drenched vine,
    Be yours and mine!

Autumnal

For Alexander Teixeira de Mattos

Pale amber sunlight falls across
    The reddening October trees,
    That hardly sway before a breeze
As soft as summer: summer's loss
    Seems little, dear! on days like these!

Let misty autumn be our part!
    The twilight of the year is sweet:
    Where shadow and the darkness meet
Our love, a twilight of the heart
    Eludes a little time's deceit.

Are we not better and at home
　　In dreamful Autumn, we who deem
　　No harvest joy is worth a dream?
A little while and night shall come,
　　A little while, then, let us dream.

Beyond the pearled horizons lie
　　Winter and night: awaiting these
　　We garner this poor hour of ease,
Until love turn from us and die
　　Beneath the drear November trees.

Villanelle of His Lady's Treasures

I took her dainty eyes, as well
　　As silken tendrils of her hair:
And so I made a Villanelle!

I took her voice, a silver bell,
　　As clear as song, as soft as prayer;
I took her dainty eyes as well.

It may be, said I, who can tell,
　　These things shall be my less despair?
And so I made a Villanelle!

I took her whiteness virginal
　　And from her cheek two roses rare:
I took her dainty eyes as well.

I said: 'It may be possible
　　Her image from my heart to tear!'
And so I made a Villanelle.

I stole her laugh, most musical:
　　I wrought it in with artful care;
I took her dainty eyes as well;
And so I made a Villanelle.

Gray Nights

For Charles Sayle

Awhile we wandered (thus it is I dream!)
Through a long, sandy track of No Man's Land,
Where only poppies grew among the sand,
The which we, plucking, cast with scant esteem,
And ever sadlier, into the sad stream,
Which followed us, as we went, hand in hand,
Under the estrangèd stars, a road unplanned,
Seeing all things in the shadow of a dream.
And ever sadlier, as the stars expired,
We found the poppies rarer, till thine eyes
Grown all my light, to light me were too tired,
And at their darkening, that no surmise
Might haunt me of the lost days we desired,
After them all I flung those memories!

Vesperal

For Hubert Crackanthorpe

Strange grows the river on the sunless evenings!
The river comforts me, grown spectral, vague and dumb:
Long was the day; at last the consoling shadows come:
Sufficient for the day are the day's evil things!

Labour and longing and despair the long day brings;
Patient till evening men watch the sun go west;
Deferred, expected night at last brings sleep and rest:
Sufficient for the day are the day's evil things!

At last the tranquil Angelus of evening rings
Night's curtain down for comfort and oblivion
Of all the vanities observèd by the sun:
Sufficient for the day are the day's evil things!

So, some time, when the last of all our evenings
Crowneth memorially the last of all our days,
Not loth to take his poppies man goes down and says,
'Sufficient for the day were the day's evil things!'

The Garden of Shadow

Love heeds no more the sighing of the wind
Against the perfect flowers: thy garden's close
Is grown a wilderness, where none shall find
One strayed, last petal of one last year's rose.

O bright, bright hair! O mouth like a ripe fruit!
Can famine be so nigh to harvesting?
Love, that was songful, with a broken lute
In grass of graveyards goeth murmuring.

Let the wind blow against the perfect flowers,
And all thy garden change and glow with spring:
Love is grown blind with no more count of hours,
Nor part in seed-time nor in harvesting.

Soli Cantare Periti Arcades

For Aubrey Beardsley

Oh, I would live in a dairy,
  And its Colin I would be,
And many a rustic fairy
  Should churn the milk with me.

Or the fields should be my pleasure,
  And my flocks should follow me,
Piping a frolic measure
  For Joan or Marjorie.

For the town is black and weary,
    And I hate the London street;
But the country ways are cheery,
    And country lanes are sweet.

Good luck to you, Paris ladies!
    Ye are over fine and nice,
I know where the country maid is,
    Who needs not asking twice.

Ye are brave in your silks and satins,
    As ye mince about the Town;
But her feet go free in pattens,
    If she wear a russet gown.

If she be not queen nor goddess
    She shall milk my brown-eyed herds,
And the breasts beneath her boddice
    Are whiter than her curds.

So I will live in a dairy,
    And its Colin I will be,
And it's Joan that I will marry,
    Or, haply, Marjorie.

On the Birth of a Friend's Child

For Victor and Nellie Plarr

Mark the day white, on which the Fates have smiled:
Eugenio and Egeria have a child.
On whom abundant grace kind Jove imparts
If she but copy either parent's parts.
Then, Muses! long devoted to her race,
Grant her Egeria's virtues and her face;
Nor stop your bounty there, but add to it
Eugenio's learning and Eugenio's wit.

Extreme Unction

For Lionel Johnson

Upon the eyes, the lips, the feet,
   On all the passages of sense,
The atoning oil is spread with sweet
   Renewal of lost innocence.

The feet, that lately ran so fast
   To meet desire, are soothly sealed;
The eyes, that were so often cast
   On vanity, are touched and healed.

From troublous sights and sounds set free;
   In such a twilight hour of breath,
Shall one retrace his life, or see,
   Through shadows, the true face of death?

Vials of mercy! Sacring oils!
   I know not where nor when I come,
Nor through what wanderings and toils,
   To crave of you Viaticum.

Yet, when the walls of flesh grow weak,
   In such an hour, it well may be,
Through mist and darkness, light will break,
   And each anointed sense will see.

A Valediction

If we must part,
   Then let it be like this;
Not heart on heart,
   Nor with the useless anguish of a kiss;
But touch mine hand and say;
'Until tomorrow or some other day,
   If we must part.'

Words are so weak
  When love hath been so strong:
Let silence speak:
  'Life is a little while, and love is long;
A time to sow and reap,
And after harvest a long time to sleep,
  But words are weak.'

Sapientia Lunae

For André Lebey

The wisdom of the world said unto me:
  'Go forth and run, the race is to the brave;
Perchance some honour tarrieth for thee!'
  'As tarrieth,' I said, 'for sure, the grave.'
    For I had pondered on a rune of roses,
    Which to her votaries the moon discloses.

The wisdom of the world said: *'There are bays:*
  Go forth and run, for victory is good,
After the stress of the laborious days.'
  'Yet,' said I, 'shall I be the worms' sweet food,'
    As I went musing on a rune of roses,
    Which in her hour, the pale, soft moon discloses.

Then said my voices: *'Wherefore strive or run,*
  On dusty highways ever, a vain race?
The long night cometh, starless, void of sun,
  What light shall serve thee like her golden face?'
    For I had pondered on a rune of roses,
    And knew some secrets which the moon discloses.

'Yea,' said I, 'for her eyes are pure and sweet
  As lilies, and the fragrance of her hair
Is many laurels; and it is not meet
  To run for shadows when the prize is here;'
    And I went reading in that rune of roses
    Which to her votaries the moon discloses.

'Cease smiling, Dear! a little while be sad'

Dum nos fata sinunt, oculos satiemus Amore.
PROPERTIUS

Cease smiling, Dear! a little while be sad,
   Here in the silence, under the wan moon;
Sweet are thine eyes, but how can I be glad,
     Knowing they change so soon?

For Love's sake, Dear, be silent! Cover me
   In the deep darkness of thy falling hair:
Fear is upon me and the memory
     Of what is all men's share.

O could this moment be perpetuate!
   Must we grow old, and leaden-eyed and gray,
And taste no more the wild and passionate
     Love sorrows of today?

Grown old, and faded, Sweet! and past desire,
   Let memory die, lest there be too much ruth,
Remembering the old, extinguished fire
     Of our divine, lost youth.

O red pomegranate of thy perfect mouth!
   My lips' life-fruitage, might I taste and die,
Here in thy garden, where the scented south
     Wind chastens agony;

Reap death from thy live lips in one long kiss,
   And look my last into thine eyes and rest:
What sweets had life to me sweeter than this
     Swift dying on thy breast?

Or, if that may not be, for Love's sake, Dear!
   Keep silence still, and dream that we shall lie,
Red mouth to mouth, entwined, and always hear
     The south wind's melody,

Here in thy garden, through the sighing boughs,
    Beyond the reach of time and chance and change,
And bitter life and death, and broken vows,
    That sadden and estrange.

Epigram

Because I am idolatrous and have besought,
With grievous supplication and consuming prayer,
The admirable image that my dreams have wrought
Out of her swan's neck and her dark, abundant hair:
The jealous gods, who brook no worship save their own,
Turned my live idol marble and her heart to stone.

Quid Non Speremus, Amantes?

For Arthur Moore

Why is there in the least touch of her hands
    More grace than other women's lips bestow,
If love is but a slave in fleshly bands
    Of flesh to flesh, wherever love may go?

Why choose vain grief and heavy-hearted hours
    For her lost voice, and dear remembered hair,
If love may cull his honey from all flowers,
    And girls grow thick as violets, everywhere?

Nay! She is gone, and all things fall apart;
    Or she is cold, and vainly have we prayed;
And broken is the summer's splendid heart,
    And hope within a deep, dark grave is laid.

As man aspires and falls, yet a soul springs
    Out of his agony of flesh at last,
So love that flesh enthralls, shall rise on wings
    Soul-centred, when the rule of flesh is past.

Then, most High Love, or wreathed with myrtle sprays
  Or crownless and forlorn, nor less a star,
Thee may I serve and follow, all my days,
  Whose thorns are sweet as never roses are!

Chanson sans Paroles

In the deep violet air,
  Not a leaf is stirred;
  There is no sound heard,
But afar, the rare
  Trilled voice of a bird.

Is the wood's dim heart,
  And the fragrant pine,
  Incense, and a shrine
Of her coming? Apart,
  I wait for a sign.

What the sudden hush said,
  She will hear, and forsake,
  Swift, for my sake,
Her green, grassy bed:
  She will hear and awake!

She will hearken and glide,
  From her place of deep rest,
  Dove-eyed, with the breast
Of a dove, to my side:
  The pines bow their crest.

I wait for a sign:
  The leaves to be waved,
  The tall tree-tops laved
In a flood of sunshine,
  This world to be saved!

In the deep violet air,
  Not a leaf is stirred;
  There is no sound heard,
But afar, the rare
  Trilled voice of a bird.

From *The Pierrot of the Minute*

The Moon Maiden's Song

Sleep!   Cast thy canopy
    Over this sleeper's brain,
Dim grow his memory,
    When he awake again.

Love stays a summer night,
    Till lights of morning come;
Then takes her wingèd flight
    Back to her starry home.

Sleep!   Yet thy days are mine;
    Love's seal is over thee:
Far though my ways from thine,
    Dim though thy memory.

Love stays a summer night,
    Till lights of morning come;
Then takes her wingèd flight
    Back to her starry home.

(When the song is finished, the curtain falls upon Pierrot sleeping.)

From *Decorations*

Beyond

Love's aftermath! I think the time is now
That we must gather in, alone, apart
The saddest crop of all the crops that grow,
   Love's aftermath.
Ah, sweet, – sweet yesterday, the tears that start
Can not put back the dial; this is, I trow,
Our harvesting! Thy kisses chill my heart,
Our lips are cold; averted eyes avow
The twilight of poor love: we can but part,
Dumbly and sadly, reaping as we sow,
   Love's aftermath.

Carthusians

Through what long heaviness, assayed in what strange fire,
   Have these white monks been brought into the way of peace,
Despising the world's wisdom and the world's desire,
   Which from the body of this death bring no release?

Within their austere walls no voices penetrate;
   A sacred silence only, as of death, obtains;
Nothing finds entry here of loud or passionate;
   This quiet is the exceeding profit of their pains.

From many lands they came, in divers fiery ways;
   Each knew at last the vanity of earthly joys;
And one was crowned with thorns, and one was crowned with bays,
   And each was tired at last of the world's foolish noise.

It was not theirs with Dominic to preach God's holy wrath,
   They were too stern to bear sweet Francis' gentle sway;
Theirs was a higher calling and a steeper path,
   To dwell alone with Christ, to meditate and pray.

A cloistered company, they are companionless,
    None knoweth here the secret of his brother's heart:
They are but come together for more loneliness,
    Whose bond is solitude and silence all their part.

O beatific life! Who is there shall gainsay,
    Your great refusal's victory, your little loss,
Deserting vanity for the more perfect way,
    The sweeter service of the most dolorous Cross.

Ye shall prevail at last! Surely ye shall prevail!
    Your silence and austerity shall win at last:
Desire and mirth, the world's ephemeral lights shall fail,
    The sweet star of your queen is never overcast.

We fling up flowers and laugh, we laugh across the wine;
    With wine we dull our souls and careful strains of art;
Our cups are polished skulls round which the roses twine:
    None dares to look at Death who leers and lurks apart.

Move on, white company, whom that has not sufficed!
    Our viols cease, our wine is death, our roses fail:
Pray for our heedlessness, O dwellers with the Christ!
    Though the world fall apart, surely ye shall prevail.

The Three Witches

All the moon-shed nights are over,
    And the days of gray and dun;
There is neither may nor clover,
    And the day and night are one.

Not an hamlet, not a city
    Meets our strained and tearless eyes;
In the plain without a pity,
    Where the wan grass droops and dies.

We shall wander through the meaning
Of a day and see no light,
For our lichened arms are leaning
On the ends of endless night.

We, the children of Astarte,
Dear abortions of the moon,
In a gay and silent party,
We are riding to you soon.

Burning ramparts, ever burning!
To the flame which never dies
We are yearning, yearning, yearning,
With our gay and tearless eyes.

In the plain without a pity,
(Not an hamlet, not a city)
Where the wan grass droops and dies.

Villanelle of the Poet's Road

Wine and woman and song,
Three things garnish our way:
Yet is day over long.

Lest we do our youth wrong,
Gather them while we may:
Wine and woman and song.

Three things render us strong,
Vine leaves, kisses and bay;
Yet is day over long.

Unto us they belong,
Us the bitter and gay,
Wine and woman and song.

We, as we pass along,
    Are sad that they will not stay;
Yet is day over long.

Fruits and flowers among,
    What is better than they:
Wine and woman and song?
    Yet is day over long.

Villanelle of Acheron

By the pale marge of Acheron,
    Methinks we shall pass restfully,
Beyond the scope of any sun.

There all men hie them one by one,
    Far from the stress of earth and sea,
By the pale marge of Acheron.

'Tis well when life and love is done,
    'Tis very well at last to be,
Beyond the scope of any sun.

No busy voices there shall stun
    Our ears: the stream flows silently
By the pale marge of Acheron.

There is the crown of labour won,
    The sleep of immortality,
Beyond the scope of any sun.

Life, of thy gifts I will have none,
    My queen is that Persephone,
By the pale marge of Acheron,
    Beyond the scope of any sun.

Saint Germain-en-Laye
(1887–95)

Through the green boughs I hardly saw thy face,
They twined so close: the sun was in mine eyes;
And now the sullen trees in sombre lace
Stand bare beneath the sinister, sad skies.

O sun and summer! Say in what far night,
The gold and green, the glory of thine head,
Of bough and branch have fallen? Oh, the white
Gaunt ghosts that flutter where thy feet have sped,

Across the terrace that is desolate,
And rang then with thy laughter, ghost of thee,
That holds its shroud up with most delicate,
Dead fingers, and behind the ghost of me,

Tripping fantastic with a mouth that jeers
At roseal flowers of youth the turbid streams
Toss in derision down the barren years
To death the host of all our golden dreams.

After Paul Verlaine

I

Il pleut doucement sur la ville.
RIMBAUD

Tears fall within mine heart,
As rain upon the town:
Whence does this languor start,
Possessing all mine heart?

O sweet fall of the rain
Upon the earth and roofs!
Unto an heart in pain,
O music of the rain!

Tears that have no reason
Fall in my sorry heart:
What! there was no treason?
This grief hath no reason.

Nay! the more desolate,
Because, I know not why,
(Neither for love nor hate)
Mine heart is desolate.

II: Colloque Sentimental

Into the lonely park all frozen fast,
A while ago there were two forms who passed.

Lo, are their lips fallen and their eyes dead,
Hardly shall a man hear the words they said.

Into the lonely park, all frozen fast,
There came two shadows who recall the past.

'Dost thou remember our old ecstasy?' –
'Wherefore should I possess that memory?' –

'Doth thine heart beat at my sole name alway?
Still dost thou see my soul in visions?' 'Nay!' –

'They were fair days of joy unspeakable,
Whereon our lips were joined?' – 'I cannot tell.' –

'Were not the heavens blue, was not hope high?' –
'Hope has fled vanquished down the darkling sky.' –

So through the barren oats they wandered,
And the night only heard the words they said.

III: Spleen

Around were all the roses red,
The ivy all around was black,

Dear, so thou only move thine head,
Shall all mine old despairs awake!

Too blue, too tender was the sky,
The air too soft, too green the sea.

Always I fear, I know not why,
Some lamentable flight from thee.

I am so tired of holly-sprays
And weary of the bright box-tree,

Of all the endless country ways;
Of everything alas! save thee.

IV

The sky is up above the roof
    So blue, so soft!
A tree there, up above the roof,
    Swayeth aloft.

A bell within that sky we see,
    Chimes low and faint:
A bird upon that tree we see,
    Maketh complaint.

Dear God! is not the life up there,
    Simple and sweet?
How peacefully are borne up there
    Sounds of the street!

What hast thou done, who comest here,
    To weep alway?
Where hast thou laid, who comest here,
    Thy youth away?

To His Mistress

There comes an end to summer,
    To spring showers and hoar rime;
His mumming to each mummer
    Has somewhere end in time,
And since life ends and laughter,
    And leaves fall and tears dry,
Who shall call love immortal,
    When all that is must die?

Nay, sweet, let's leave unspoken
    The vows the fates gainsay,
For all vows made are broken,
    We love but while we may.
Let's kiss when kissing pleases,
    And part when kisses pall,
Perchance, this time tomorrow,
    We shall not love at all.

You ask my love completest,
    As strong next year as now,
The devil take you, sweetest,
    Ere I make aught such vow.
Life is a masque that changes,
    A fig for constancy!
No love at all were better,
    Than love which is not free.

In a Breton Cemetery

They sleep well here,
   These fisher-folk who passed their anxious days
   In fierce Atlantic ways;
And found not there,
   Beneath the long curled wave,
   So quiet a grave.

And they sleep well
   These peasant-folk, who told their lives away,
   From day to market-day,
As one should tell,
   With patient industry,
   Some sad old rosary.

And now night falls,
   Me, tempest-tost, and driven from pillar to post,
   A poor worn ghost,
This quiet pasture calls;
   And dear dead people with pale hands
   Beckon me to their lands.

To William Theodore Peters on His Renaissance Cloak

The cherry-coloured velvet of your cloak
   Time hath not soiled: its fair embroideries
Gleam as when centuries ago they spoke
   To what bright gallant of Her Daintiness,
   Whose slender fingers, long since dust and dead,
   For love or courtesy embroidered
The cherry-coloured velvet of this cloak.

Ah! cunning flowers of silk and silver thread,
    That mock mortality! the broidering dame,
The page they decked, the kings and courts are dead:
    Gone the age beautiful; Lorenzo's name,
    The Borgia's pride are but an empty sound;
    But lustrous still upon their velvet ground,
Time spares these flowers of silk and silver thread.

Gone is that age of pageant and of pride:
    Yet don your cloak, and haply it shall seem,
The curtain of old time is set aside;
    As through the sadder coloured throng you gleam;
    We see once more fair dame and gallant gay,
    The glamour and the grace of yesterday:
The elder, brighter age of pomp and pride.

Dregs

The fire is out, and spent the warmth thereof,
(This is the end of every song man sings!)
The golden wine is drunk, the dregs remain,
Bitter as wormwood and as salt as pain;
And health and hope have gone the way of love
Into the drear oblivion of lost things.
Ghosts go along with us until the end;
This was a mistress, this, perhaps, a friend.
With pale, indifferent eyes, we sit and wait
For the dropt curtain and the closing gate:
This is the end of all the songs man sings.

A Song

All that a man may pray,
    Have I not prayed to thee?
What were praise left to say,
    Has not been said by me,
        O, *ma mie?*

Yet thine eyes and thine heart,
  Always were dumb to me:
Only to be my part,
  Sorrow has come from thee,
    O, ma mie?

Where shall I seek and hide
  My grief away with me?
Lest my bitter tears should chide,
  Bring brief dismay to thee,
    O, ma mie?

More than a man may pray,
  Have I not prayed to thee?
What were praise left to say,
  Has not been said by me,
    O, ma mie?

Breton Afternoon

Here, where the breath of the scented-gorse floats through the
                                          sun-stained air,
On a steep hill-side, on a grassy ledge, I have lain hours long and
                                                        heard
Only the faint breeze pass in a whisper like a prayer,
And the river ripple by and the distant call of a bird.

On the lone hill-side, in the gold sunshine, I will hush me and
                                                  repose,
And the world fades into a dream and a spell is cast on me;
And what was all the strife about, for the myrtle or the rose,
And why have I wept for a white girl's paleness passing ivory!

Out of the tumult of angry tongues, in a land alone, apart,
In a perfumed dream-land set betwixt the bounds of life and death,
Here will I lie while the clouds fly by and delve an hole where my
heart
May sleep deep down with the gorse above and red, red earth
beneath.

Sleep and be quiet for an afternoon, till the rose-white angelus
Softly steals my way from the village under the hill:
Mother of God, O Misericord, look down in pity on us,
The weak and blind who stand in our light and wreak ourselves such ill.

Venite Descendamus

Let be at last; give over words and sighing,
　　Vainly were all things said:
Better at last to find a place for lying,
　　Only dead.

Silence were best, with songs and sighing over;
　　Now be the music mute;
Now let the dead, red leaves of autumn cover
　　A vain lute.

Silence is best: for ever and for ever,
　　We will go down and sleep,
Somewhere beyond her ken, where she need never
　　Come to weep.

Let be at last: colder she grows and colder;
　　Sleep and the night were best;
Lying at last where we cannot behold her,
　　We may rest.

Transition

A little while to walk with thee, dear child;
  To lean on thee my weak and weary head;
Then evening comes: the winter sky is wild,
  The leafless trees are black, the leaves long dead.

A little while to hold thee and to stand,
  By harvest-fields of bending golden corn:
Then the predestined silence, and thine hand,
  Lost in the night, long and weary and forlorn.

A little while to love thee, scarcely time
  To love thee well enough; then time to part,
To fare through wintry fields alone and climb
  The frozen hills, not knowing where thou art.

Short summer-time and then, my heart's desire,
  The winter and the darkness: one by one
The roses fall, the pale roses expire
  Beneath the slow decadence of the sun.

Exchanges

All that I had I brought,
  Little enough I know;
A poor rhyme roughly wrought,
  A rose to match thy snow:
All that I had I brought.

Little enough I sought:
  But a word compassionate,
A passing glance, or thought,
  For me outside the gate:
Little enough I sought.

Little enough I found:
    All that you had, perchance!
With the dead leaves on the ground,
    I dance the devil's dance.
All that you had I found.

To a Lady Asking Foolish Questions

Why am I sorry, Chloe? Because the moon is far:
And who am I to be straitened in a little earthly star?

Because thy face is fair? And what if it had not been,
The fairest face of all is the face I have not seen.

Because the land is cold, and however I scheme and plot,
I can not find a ferry to the land where I am not.

Because thy lips are red and thy breasts upbraid the snow?
(There is neither white nor red in the pleasance where I go.)

Because thy lips grow pale and thy breasts grow dun and fall?
I go where the wind blows, Chloe, and am not sorry at all.

Rondeau

Ah, Manon, say, why is it we
Are one and all so fain of thee?
Thy rich red beauty debonnaire
In very truth is not more fair,
Than the shy grace and purity
That clothe the maiden maidenly;
Her gray eyes shine more tenderly
And not less bright than thine her hair,
    Ah, Manon, say!
Expound, I pray, the mystery
Why wine-stained lip and languid eye,
And most unsaintly Maenad air,
Should move us more than all the rare
White roses of virginity?
    Ah, Manon, say!

Moritura

A song of the setting sun!
  The sky in the west is red,
And the day is all but done:
  While yonder up overhead,
    All too soon,
There rises, so cold, the cynic moon.

A song of a winter day!
  The wind of the north doth blow,
From a sky that's chill and gray,
  On fields where no crops now grow,
    Fields long shorn
Of bearded barley and golden corn.

A song of an old, old man!
  His hairs are white and his gaze,
Long bleared in his visage wan,
  With its weight of yesterdays,
    Joylessly
He stands and mumbles and looks at me.

A song of a faded flower!
  'Twas plucked in the tender bud,
And fair and fresh for an hour,
  In a lady's hair it stood.
    Now, ah, now,
Faded it lies in the dust and low.

Libera Me

Goddess the laughter-loving, Aphrodite befriend!
Long have I served thine altars, serve me now at the end,
Let me have peace of thee, truce of thee, golden one, send.

Heart of my heart have I offered thee, pain of my pain,
Yielding my life for the love of thee into thy chain;
Lady and goddess be merciful, loose me again.

All things I had that were fairest, my dearest and best,
Fed the fierce flames on thine altar: ah, surely, my breast
Shrined thee alone among goddesses, spurning the rest.

Blossom of youth thou hast plucked of me, flower of my days;
Stinted I nought in thine honouring, walked in thy ways,
Song of my soul pouring out to thee, all in thy praise.

Fierce was the flame while it lasted, and strong was thy wine,
Meet for immortals that die not, for throats such as thine,
Too fierce for bodies of mortals, too potent for mine.

Blossom and bloom hast thou taken, now render to me
Ashes of life that remain to me, few though they be,
Truce of the love of thee, Cyprian, let me go free.

Goddess, the laughter-loving, Aphrodite, restore
Life to the limbs of me, liberty, hold me no more
Having the first-fruits and flower of me, cast me the core.

A Last Word

Let us go hence: the night is now at hand;
The day is overworn, the birds all flown;
And we have reaped the crops the gods have sown;
Despair and death; deep darkness o'er the land,
Broods like an owl; we cannot understand
Laughter or tears, for we have only known
Surpassing vanity: vain things alone
Have driven our perverse and aimless band.
Let us go hence, somewhither strange and cold,
To Hollow Lands where just men and unjust
Find end of labour, where's rest for the old,
Freedom to all from love and fear and lust.
Twine our torn hands! O pray the earth enfold
Our life-sick hearts and turn them into dust.

Markets

After an Old Nursery Rhyme

'Where are you going, beautiful maiden?'

'I am going to market, sir.'

'And what do you take with you, beautiful maiden? Lilies out of your garden? White milk, warm from the cow, little pats of yellow butter, new-laid eggs, this morning's mushrooms? Where is your basket? Why have you nothing in your hands?'

'I am going to market, sir.'

'Beautiful maiden, may I come with you?'

'Oh, sir.'

Absinthia Taetra

Green changed to white, emerald to an opal: nothing was changed.

The man let the water trickle gently into his glass, and as the green clouded, a mist fell away from his mind.

Then he drank opaline.

Memories and terrors beset him. The past tore after him like a panther and through the blackness of the present he saw the luminous tiger eyes of the things to be.

But he drank opaline.

And that obscure night of the soul, and the valley of humiliation, through which he stumbled were forgotten. He saw blue vistas of undiscovered countries, high prospects and a quiet, caressing sea. The past shed its perfume over him, today held his hand as it were a little child, and tomorrow shone like a white star: nothing was changed.

He drank opaline.

The man had known the obscure night of the soul, and lay even now in the valley of humiliation; and the tiger menace of the things to be was red in the skies. But for a little while he had forgotten.

Green changed to white, emerald to an opal: nothing was changed.

'Because my life is an unworthy thing'

Discedam, explebo numerum, reddarque tenebris,
I decus, i, nostrum; melioribus utere fatis.

Because my life is an unworthy thing
Outworn and mildewed, I am dismayed,
I dare not give it thee, O child! O maid!
Too late divined, too sweet for me to sing:
Surely, my barren days I may not bring,
But rather giftless come, lest any shade
Or prescience of autumn should be laid
Upon thy fair life in its blossoming.
Yet would I give thee all, who stand aside,
Giving thee naught: yea! gladly lie down dead
That haply coming, where the roads divide
On lilies still thy tender feet might tread,
In daisied ways of innocence abide,
Until thy tale of days is reckoned.

[1891]

Against My Lady Burton: On Her Burning the Last Writing of Her Dead Husband

'To save his soul', whom narrowly she loved
She did this deed of everlasting shame,
For devils' laughter; and was soulless proved
Heaping dishonour on her scholar's name.
Her lean distrust awoke when he was dead;
Dead, hardly cold; whose life was worn away
In scholarship's high service; from his head
She lightly tore his ultimate crown of bay.

His masterpiece, the ripe fruit of his age,
In art's despite she gave the hungry flame;
Smiled at the death of each laborious page,
Which she read only by the light of shame.
Dying he trusted her: him dead she paid
Most womanly, destroying his life's prize:
So Judas decently his Lord betrayed
With deep dishonour wrought in love's disguise.
With deep dishonour, for her jealous heart
His whole life's work, with light excuse put by
For love of him, or haply, hating art.
Oh Love be this, let us curse Love and die.
Nay! Love forgive: could such a craven thing
Love anywhere? but let her name pass down
Dishonoured through the ages, who did fling
To the rank scented mob a sage's crown,
And offered Fame, Love, Honour, mincingly
To her one God—sterile Propriety!

[1891]

A Letter from M.M. Versified out
of Poor Prose into Catchpenny Verse!

Dear Sir! would you be popular,
   Then never mention Greek!
Be arrogant and insular,
   Dear Sir, would you be popular:
Cut classics; and for guiding star,
Read Birrell once a week.
Dear Sir! would you be popular,
   Then never mention Greek.
                                 Lionel Johnson

[This is described by Sir Desmond Flower as 'translated by Dowson
from an unpublished triolet by Lionel Johnson, which presumably
would have been in Latin or ironically in Greek'.]

Fantasie Triste

To my first love
Loved all above;
In late spring;
Pansies, pansies
Such strange fancies
Was all I had to bring.

To my last love
Loved all above:
At evening
Of autumn
One chrysanthemum
Is all I have to bring.

O first, be last
In a dim past!
With the dead flowers
And the strayed hours
There are no flowers left to bring
There are no songs left to sing
Let be at last.

Lionel Johnson

From *Poems*

Winchester

To the fairest!
        Then to thee
Consecrate and bounden be,
Winchester! this verse of mine.
Ah, that loveliness of thine!
To have lived enchaunted years
Free from sorrows, free from fears,
Where thy Tower's great shadow falls
Over those proud buttressed walls;
Whence a purpling glory pours
From high heaven's inheritors,
Throned within the arching stone!
To have wandered, hushed, alone,
Gently round thy fair, fern-grown
Chauntry of the Lilies, lying
Where the soft night winds go sighing
Round thy Cloisters, in moonlight
Branching dark, or touched with white:
Round old, chill aisles, where moon-smitten
Blanches the *Orate*, written
Under each worn, old-world face
Graven on Death's holy place!

To the noblest!
        None but thee.
Blest our living eyes, that see
Half a thousand years fulfilled
Of that age, which Wykeham willed

Thee to win; yet all unworn,
As upon that first March morn,
When thine honoured city saw
Thy young beauty without flaw,
Born within her water-flowing,
Ancient hollows, by wind-blowing
Hills enfolded ever more.
Thee, that lord of splendid lore,
Orient from old Hellas' shore,
Grocyn, had to mother: thee,
Monumental majesty
Of most high philosophy
Honours, in thy wizard Browne:
Tender Otway's dear renown,
Mover of a perfect pity,
Victim of the iron city,
Thine to cherish is: and thee,
Laureate of Liberty;
Harper of the Highland faith,
Elf, and faery, and wan wraith;
Chaunting softly, chaunting slowly,
Minstrel of all melancholy;
Master of all melody,
Made to cling round memory;
Passion's poet, Evening's voice,
Collins glorified. Rejoice,
Mother! in thy sons: for all
Love thine immemorial
Name, august and musical.
Not least he, who left thy side,
For his sire's, thine earlier pride,
Arnold: whom we mourn today,
Prince of song, and gone away
To his brothers of the bay:
Thine the love of all his years;
His be now thy praising tears.

To the dearest!
        Ah, to thee!
Hast thou not in all to me
Mother, more than mother, been?
Well toward thee may Mary Queen
Bend her with a mother's mien;
Who so rarely dost express
An inspiring tenderness,
Woven with thy sterner strain,
Prelude of the world's true pain.
But two years, and still my feet
Found thy very stones more sweet,
Than the richest fields elsewhere:
Two years, and thy sacred air
Still poured balm upon me, when
Nearer drew the world of men;
When the passions, one by one,
All sprang upward to the sun:
Two years have I lived, still thine;
Lost, thy presence! gone, that shrine,
Where six years, what years! were mine.
Music is the thought of thee;
Fragrance, all thy memory.
Those thy rugged Chambers old,
In their gloom and rudeness, hold
Dear remembrances of gold.
Some first blossoming of flowers
Made delight of all the hours;
Greatness, beauty, all things fair
Made the spirit of thine air:
Old years live with thee; thy sons
Walk with high companions.
Then, the natural joy of earth,
Joy of very health and birth!
Hills, upon a summer noon:
Water Meads, on eves of June:
Chamber Court, beneath the moon:
Days of spring, on Twyford Down,

Or when autumn woods grew brown;
As they looked, when here came Keats
Chaunting of autumnal sweets;
Through this city of old haunts,
Murmuring immortal chaunts;
As when Pope, art's earlier king,
Here, a child, did nought but sing;
Sang, a child, by nature's rule,
Round the trees of Twyford School:
Hours of sun beside Meads' Wall,
Ere the may began to fall;
Watching the rooks rise and soar,
High from lime and sycamore:
Wanderings by old-world ways,
Walks and streets of ancient days;
Closes, churches, arches, halls,
Vanished men's memorials.
There was beauty, there was grace,
Each place was an holy place:
There the kindly fates allowed
Me too room; and made me proud,
Prouder name I have not wist!
With the name of Wykehamist.
These thy joys: and more than these:
Ah, to watch beneath thy trees,
Through long twilights linden-scented,
Sunsets, lingering, lamented,
In the purple west; prevented,
Ere they fell, by evening star!
Ah, long nights of Winter! far
Leaps and roars the faggot fire;
Ruddy smoke rolls higher, higher,
Broken through by flame's desire;
Circling faces glow, all eyes
Take the light; deep radiance flies,
Merrily flushing overhead
Names of brothers, long since fled;
And fresh clusters, in their stead,

Jubilant round fierce forest flame.
Friendship too must make her claim:
But what songs, what memories end,
When they tell of friend on friend?
And for them, I thank thy name.

Love alone of gifts, no shame
Lessens, and I love thee: yet
Sound it but of echoes, let
This my maiden music be,
Of the love I bear to thee,
Witness and interpreter,
Mother mine: loved Winchester!

To Morfydd

A voice on the winds,
A voice by the waters,
  Wanders and cries:
Oh! what are the winds?
And what are the waters?
  Mine are your eyes!

Western the winds are,
And western the waters,
  Where the light lies:
Oh! what are the winds?
And what are the waters?
  Mine are your eyes!

Cold, cold, grow the winds,
And wild grow the waters,
  Where the sun dies:
Oh! what are the winds?
And what are the waters?
  Mine are your eyes!

And down the night winds,
And down the night waters,
   The music flies:
Oh! what are the winds?
And what are the waters?
Cold be the winds,
And wild be the waters,
   So mine be your eyes!

Plato in London

To Campbell Dodgson

The pure flame of one taper fall
Over the old and comely page:
No harsher light disturb at all
This converse with a treasured sage.
Seemly, and fair, and of the best,
   If Plato be our guest,
   Should things befall.

Without, a world of noise and cold:
Here, the soft burning of the fire.
And Plato walks, where heavens unfold,
About the home of his desire.
From his own city of high things,
   He shows to us, and brings,
   Truth of fine gold.

The hours pass; and the fire burns low;
The clear flame dwindles into death:
Shut then the book with care; and so,
Take leave of Plato, with hushed breath.
A little, by the falling gleams,
   Tarry the gracious dreams:
   And they too go.

Lean from the window to the air:
Hear London's voice upon the night!
Thou hast held converse with things rare:
Look now upon another sight!
The calm stars, in their living skies:
    And then, these surging cries,
    This restless glare!

That starry music, starry fire,
High above all our noise and glare:
The image of our long desire,
The beauty, and the strength, are there.
And Plato's thought lives, true and clear,
    In as august a sphere:
    Perchance, far higher.

A Friend

To H. B. Irving

All, that he came to give,
He gave, and went again:
I have seen one man live,
I have seen one man reign,
With all the graces in his train.

As one of us, he wrought
Things of the common hour:
Whence was the charmed soul brought,
That gave each act such power;
The natural beauty of a flower?

Magnificence and grace,
Excellent courtesy:
A brightness on the face,
Airs of high memory:
Whence came all these, to such as he?

Like young Shakespearian kings,
He won the adoring throng:
And, as Apollo sings,
He triumphed with a song:
Triumphed, and sang, and passed along.

With a light word, he took
The hearts of men in thrall:
And, with a golden look,
Welcomed them, at his call
Giving their love, their strength, their all.

No man less proud than he,
Nor cared for homage less:
Only, he could not be
Far off from happiness:
Nature was bound to his success.

Weary, the cares, the jars,
The lets, of every day:
But the heavens filled with stars,
Chanced he upon the way:
And where he stayed, all joy would stay.

Now, when sad night draws down,
When the austere stars burn:
Roaming the vast live town,
My thoughts and memories yearn
Toward him, who never will return.

Yet have I seen him live,
And owned my friend, a king:
All that he came to give,
He gave: and I, who sing
His praise, bring all I have to bring.

By the Statue of King Charles at Charing Cross

To William Watson

Sombre and rich, the skies;
Great glooms, and starry plains.
Gently the night wind sighs;
Else a vast silence reigns.

The splendid silence clings
Around me: and around
The saddest of all kings
Crowned, and again discrowned.

Comely and calm, he rides
Hard by his own Whitehall:
Only the night wind glides:
No crowds, nor rebels, brawl.

Gone, too, his Court: and yet,
The stars his courtiers are:
Stars in their stations set;
And every wandering star.

Alone he rides, alone,
The fair and fatal king:
Dark night is all his own,
That strange and solemn thing.

Which are more full of fate:
The stars; or those sad eyes?
Which are more still and great:
Those brows; or the dark skies?

Although his whole heart yearn
In passionate tragedy:
Never was face so stern
With sweet austerity.

Vanquished in life, his death
By beauty made amends:
The passing of his breath
Won his defeated ends.

Brief life, and hapless? Nay:
Through death, life grew sublime.
Speak after sentence? Yea:
And to the end of time.

Armoured he rides, his head
Bare to the stars of doom:
He triumphs now, the dead,
Beholding London's gloom.

Our wearier spirit faints,
Vexed in the world's employ:
His soul was of the saints;
And art to him was joy.

King, tried in fires of woe!
Men hunger for thy grace:
And through the night I go,
Loving thy mournful face.

Yet, when the city sleeps;
When all the cries are still:
The stars and heavenly deeps
Work out a perfect will.

The Precept of Silence

I know you: solitary griefs,
Desolate passions, aching hours!
I know you: tremulous beliefs,
Agonized hopes, and ashen flowers!

The winds are sometimes sad to me;
The starry spaces, full of fear:
Mine is the sorrow on the sea,
And mine the sigh of places drear.

Some players upon plaintive strings
Publish their wistfulness abroad:
I have not spoken of these things,
Save to one man, and unto God.

Mystic and Cavalier

To Herbert Percy Horne

Go from me: I am one of those, who fall.
What! hath no cold wind swept your heart at all,
In my sad company? Before the end,
 Go from me, dear my friend!

Yours are the victories of light: your feet
Rest from good toil, where rest is brave and sweet.
But after warfare in a mourning gloom,
 I rest in clouds of doom.

Have you not read so, looking in these eyes?
Is it the common light of the pure skies,
Lights up their shadowy depths? The end is set:
 Though the end be not yet.

When gracious music stirs, and all is bright,
And beauty triumphs through a courtly night;
When I too joy, a man like other men:
 Yet, am I like them, then?

And in the battle, when the horsemen sweep
Against a thousand deaths, and fall on sleep:
Who ever sought that sudden calm, if I
 Sought not? Yet, could not die.

Seek with thine eyes to pierce this crystal sphere:
Canst read a fate there, prosperous and clear?
Only the mists, only the weeping clouds:
    Dimness, and airy shrouds.

Beneath, what angels are at work? What powers
Prepare the secret of the fatal hours?
See! the mists tremble, and the clouds are stirred:
    When comes the calling word?

The clouds are breaking from the crystal ball,
Breaking and clearing: and I look to fall.
When the cold winds and airs of portent sweep,
    My spirit may have sleep.

O rich and sounding voices of the air!
Interpreters and prophets of despair:
Priests of a fearful sacrament! I come,
    To make with you mine home.

Parnell

To John McGrath

The wail of Irish winds,
The cry of Irish seas:
Eternal sorrow finds
Eternal voice in these.

I cannot praise our dead,
Whom Ireland weeps so well:
Her morning light, that fled;
Her morning star, that fell.

She of the mournful eyes
Waits, and no dark clouds break:
Waits, and her strong son lies
Dead, for her holy sake.

Her heart is sorrow's home,
And hath been from of old:
An host of griefs hath come,
To make that heart their fold.

Ah, the sad autumn day,
When the last sad troop came
Swift down the ancient way,
Keening a chieftain's name!

Gray hope was there, and dread;
Anger, and love in tears:
They mourned the dear and dead,
Dirge of the ruined years.

Home to her heart she drew
The mourning company:
Old sorrows met the new,
In sad fraternity.

A mother, and forget?
Nay! all her children's fate
Ireland remembers yet,
With love insatiate.

She hears the heavy bells:
Hears, and with passionate breath
Eternally she tells
A rosary of death.

Faithful and true is she,
The mother of us all:
Faithful and true! may we
Fail her not, though we fall.

Her son, our brother, lies
Dead, for her holy sake:
But from the dead arise
Voices, that bid us wake.

Not his, to hail the dawn:
His but the herald's part.
Be ours to see withdrawn
Night from our mother's heart.

Hawthorne

To Walter Alison Phillips

Ten years ago I heard; ten, have I loved;
Thine haunting voice borne over the waste sea.
Was it thy melancholy spirit moved
Mine, with those gray dreams, that invested thee?
Or was it, that thy beauty first reproved
The imperfect fancies, that looked fair to me?

Thou hast both secrets: for to thee are known
The fatal sorrows binding life and death:
And thou hast found, on winds of passage blown,
That music, which is sorrow's perfect breath:
So, all thy beauty takes a solemn tone,
And art, is all thy melancholy saith.

Now therefore is thy voice abroad for me,
When through dark woodlands murmuring sounds make way:
Thy voice, and voices of the sounding sea,
Stir in the branches, as none other may:
All pensive loneliness is full of thee,
And each mysterious, each autumnal day.

Hesperian soul! Well hadst thou in the West
Thine hermitage and meditative place:
In mild retiring fields thou wast at rest,
Calmed by old winds, touched with aërial grace:
Fields, whence old magic simples filled thy breast,
And unforgotten fragrance balmed thy face.

Glories

To Theodore Peters

Roses from Paestan rosaries!
More goodly red and white was she:
Her red and white were harmonies,
Not matched upon a Paestan tree.

Ivories blaunched in Alban air!
She lies more purely blaunched than you:
No Alban whiteness doth she wear,
But death's perfection of that hue.

Nay! now the rivalry is done,
Of red, and white, and whiter still:
She hath a glory from that sun,
Who falls not from Olympus hill.

Celtic Speech

To Dr Douglas Hyde

Never forgetful silence fall on thee,
  Nor younger voices overtake thee,
Nor echoes from thine ancient hills forsake thee;
Old music heard by Mona of the sea:
And where with moving melodies there break thee
Pastoral Conway, venerable Dee.

Like music lives, nor may that music die,
  Still in the far, fair Gaelic places:
The speech, so wistful with its kindly graces,
Holy Croagh Patrick knows, and holy Hy:
The speech, that wakes the soul in withered faces,
And wakes remembrance of great things gone by.

Like music by the desolate Land's End
   Mournful forgetfulness hath broken:
No more words kindred to the winds are spoken,
Where upon iron cliffs whole seas expend
That strength, whereof the unalterable token
Remains wild music, even to the world's end.

from Sancta Silvarum

III
Through the fresh woods there fleet
Fawns, with bright eyes, light feet:
Bright eyes, and feet that spurn
      The pure green fern.

Headed by leaping does,
The swift procession goes
Through thickets, over lawns:
      Followed by fawns.

Over slopes, over glades,
Down dells and leafy shades,
Away the quick deer troop:
      A wildwood group.

Under the forest airs,
A life of grace is theirs:
Courtly their look; they seem
      Things of a dream.

Some say, but who can say?
That a charmed troop are they:
Once youths and maidens white!
      These may be right.

Bagley Wood

To Percy Addleshaw

The night is full of stars, full of magnificence:
Nightingales hold the wood, and fragrance loads the dark.
Behold, what fires august, what lights eternal! Hark,
What passionate music poured in passionate love's defence!
Breathe but the wafting wind's nocturnal frankincense!
Only to feel this night's great heart, only to mark
The splendours and the glooms, brings back the patriarch,
Who on Chaldæan wastes found God through reverence.
Could we but live at will upon this perfect height,
Could we but always keep the passion of this peace,
Could we but face unshamed the look of this pure light,
Could we but win earth's heart, and give desire release:
Then were we all divine, and then were ours by right
These stars, these nightingales, these scents: then shame would
cease.

The Dark Angel

Dark Angel, with thine aching lust
To rid the world of penitence:
Malicious Angel, who still dost
My soul such subtile violence!

Because of thee, no thought, no thing,
Abides for me undesecrate:
Dark Angel, ever on the wing,
Who never reachest me too late!

When music sounds, then changest thou
Its silvery to a sultry fire:
Nor will thine envious heart allow
Delight untortured by desire.

103

Through thee, the gracious Muses turn
To Furies, O mine Enemy!
And all the things of beauty burn
With flames of evil ecstasy.

Because of thee, the land of dreams
Becomes a gathering place of fears:
Until tormented slumber seems
One vehemence of useless tears.

When sunlight glows upon the flowers,
Or ripples down the dancing sea:
Thou, with thy troop of passionate powers,
Beleaguerest, bewilderest, me.

Within the breath of autumn woods,
Within the winter silences:
Thy venomous spirit stirs and broods,
O Master of impieties!

The ardour of red flame is thine,
And thine the steely soul of ice:
Thou poisonest the fair design
Of nature, with unfair device.

Apples of ashes, golden bright;
Waters of bitterness, how sweet!
O banquet of a foul delight,
Prepared by thee, dark Paraclete!

Thou art the whisper in the gloom,
The hinting tone, the haunting laugh:
Thou art the adorner of my tomb,
The minstrel of mine epitaph.

I fight thee, in the Holy Name!
Yet, what thou dost, is what God saith:
Tempter! should I escape thy flame,
Thou wilt have helped my soul from Death:

The second Death, that never dies,
That cannot die, when time is dead:
Live Death, wherein the lost soul cries,
Eternally uncomforted.

Dark Angel, with thine aching lust!
Of two defeats, of two despairs:
Less dread, a change to drifting dust,
Than thine eternity of cares.

Do what thou wilt, thou shalt not so,
Dark Angel! triumph over me:
Lonely, unto the Lone I go;
Divine, to the Divinity.

A Friend

His are the whitenesses of soul,
That Virgil had: he walks the earth
A classic saint, in self-control,
And comeliness, and quiet mirth.

His presence wins me to repose:
When he is with me, I forget
All heaviness: and when he goes,
The comfort of the sun is set.

But in the lonely hours I learn,
How I can serve and thank him best:
God! trouble him: that he may turn
Through sorrow to the only rest.

To a Passionist

Clad in a vestment wrought with passion-flowers;
Celebrant of one Passion; called by name
Passionist: is thy world, one world with ours?
Thine, a like heart? Thy very soul, the same?

Thou pleadest an eternal sorrow: we
Praise the still changing beauty of this earth.
Passionate good and evil, thou dost see:
Our eyes behold the dreams of death and birth.

We love the joys of men: we love the dawn,
Red with the sun, and with the pure dew pearled.
Thy stern soul feels, after the sun withdrawn,
How much pain goes to perfecting the world.

Canst thou be right? Is thine the very truth?
Stands then our life in so forlorn a state?
Nay, but thou wrongest us: thou wrong'st our youth,
Who dost our happiness compassionate.

And yet! and yet! O royal Calvary!
Whence divine sorrow triumphed through years past:
Could ages bow before mere memory?
Those passion-flowers must blossom, to the last.

Purple they bloom, the splendour of a King:
Crimson they bleed, the sacrament of Death:
About our thrones and pleasaunces they cling,
Where guilty eyes read, what each blossom saith.

To Leo XIII

Leo! Vicar of Christ,
His voice, His love, His sword:
Leo! Vicar of Christ,
Earth's Angel of the Lord:

Leo! Father of all,
Whose are all hearts to keep:
Leo! Father of all,
Chief Shepherd of the sheep:

Leo! Lover of men,
Through all the labouring lands:
Leo! Lover of men,
Blest by thine holy hands:

Leo! Ruler of Rome,
Heir of its royal race:
Leo! Ruler of Rome,
King of the Holy Place:

Leo! Leo the Great!
Glory, and love, and fear,
Leo! Leo the Great!
We give thee, great and dear:

Leo! God grant this thing:
Might some, so proud to be
Children of England, bring
Thine England back to thee!

The Church of a Dream

To Bernhard Berenson

Sadly the dead leaves rustle in the whistling wind,
Around the weather-worn, gray church, low down the vale:
The Saints in golden vesture shake before the gale;
The glorious windows shake, where still they dwell enshrined;
Old Saints by long dead, shrivelled hands, long since designed:
There still, although the world autumnal be, and pale,
Still in their golden vesture the old saints prevail;
Alone with Christ, desolate else, left by mankind.

Only one ancient Priest offers the Sacrifice,
Murmuring holy Latin immemorial:
Swaying with tremulous hands the old censer full of spice,
In gray, sweet incense clouds; blue, sweet clouds mystical:
To him, in place of men, for he is old, suffice
Melancholy remembrances and vesperal.

The Age of a Dream

To Christopher Whall

Imageries of dreams reveal a gracious age:
Black armour, falling lace, and altar lights at morn.
The courtesy of Saints, their gentleness and scorn,
Lights on an earth more fair, than shone from Plato's page:
The courtesy of knights, fair calm and sacred rage:
The courtesy of love, sorrow for love's sake borne.
Vanished, those high conceits! Desolate and forlorn,
We hunger against hope for that lost heritage.

Gone now, the carven work! Ruined, the golden shrine!
No more the glorious organs pour their voice divine;
No more rich frankincense drifts through the Holy Place:
Now from the broken tower, what solemn bell still tolls,
Mourning what piteous death? Answer, O saddened souls!
Who mourn the death of beauty and the death of grace.

Sortes Virgilianae

To John Barlas

Lord of the Golden Branch, Virgil! and Caesar's friend:
Leader of pilgrim Dante! Yes: *things have their tears:*
So sighed thy song, when down sad winds pierced to thine ears
Wandering and immemorial sorrows without end.
And things of death touch hearts, that die: Yes: but joys blend,
And glories, with our little life of human fears:
Rome reigns, and Caesar triumphs! Ah, the Golden Years,
The Golden Years return: this also the Gods send.

O men, who have endured an heavier burden yet!
Hear you not happy airs, and voices augural?
For you, in these last days by sure foreknowledge set,
Looms no Italian shore, bright and imperial?
Wounded and worn! What Virgil sang, doth God forget?
Virgil, the melancholy, the majestical.

Consolation

Sighing and grief are all my portion now,
    Sighing and grief:
But thou art somewhere smiling: thou,
    Like a frail leaf,

By winter's mercy spared a little yet,
    Canst put aside
The coming shadow: happy to forget,
    How thy companion died.

The Destroyer of a Soul

To———.

I hate you with a necessary hate.
First, I sought patience: passionate was she:
My patience turned in very scorn of me,
That I should dare forgive a sin so great,
As this, through which I sit disconsolate;
Mourning for that live soul, I used to see;
Soul of a saint, whose friend I used to be:
Till you came by! a cold, corrupting, fate.

Why come you now? You, whom I cannot cease
With pure and perfect hate to hate? Go, ring
The death-bell with a deep, triumphant toll!
Say you, my friend sits by me still? Ah, peace!
Call you this thing my friend? this nameless thing?
This living body, hiding its dead soul?

To Certain Friends

I thank Eternal God, that you are mine,
Who are His too: courageous and divine
Must friendship be, through this great grace of God;
And have Eternity for period.

The Classics

To Ion Thynne

Fain to know golden things, fain to grow wise,
Fain to achieve the secret of fair souls:
His thought, scarce other lore need solemnize,
Whom Virgil calms, whom Sophocles controls:

Whose conscience Æschylus, a warrior voice,
Enchaunted hath with majesties of doom:
Whose melancholy mood can best rejoice,
When Horace sings, and roses bower the tomb:

Who, following Caesar unto death, discerns
What bitter cause was Rome's, to mourn that day:
With austere Tacitus for master, learns
The look of empire in its proud decay:

Whom dread Lucretius of the mighty line
Hath awed, but not borne down: who loves the flame,
That leaped within Catullus the divine,
His glory, and his beauty, and his shame:

Who dreams with Plato and, transcending dreams,
Mounts to the perfect City of true God:
Who hails its marvellous and haunting gleams,
Treading the steady air, as Plato trod:

Who with Thucydides pursues the way,
Feeling the heart-beats of the ages gone:
Till fall the clouds upon the Attic day,
And Syracuse draw tears for Marathon:

To whom these golden things best give delight:
The music of most sad Simonides;
Propertius' ardent graces; and the might
Of Pindar chaunting by the olive trees:

Livy, and Roman consuls purple swathed:
Plutarch, and heroes of the ancient earth:
And Aristophanes, whose laughter scathed
The souls of fools, and pealed in lyric mirth:

Æolian rose-leaves blown from Sappho's isle;
Secular glories of Lycean thought:
Sallies of Lucian, bidding wisdom smile;
Angers of Juvenal, divinely wrought:

Pleasant, and elegant, and garrulous,
Pliny: crowned Marcus, wistful and still strong:
Sicilian seas and their Theocritus,
Pastoral singer of the last Greek song:

Herodotus, all simple and all wise:
Demosthenes, a lightning flame of scorn:
The surge of Cicero, that never dies:
And Homer, grand against the ancient morn.

April

To Richard Le Gallienne

A pleasant heat breathes off the scented grass,
   From the bright green blades, and shining daisies:
Now give we joy, who sometime cried, Alas!
Now set we forth our melodies, and sing
    Soft praises to the spring,
      Musical praises.

The flying winds are lovely with the sun:
   Now all in sweet and dainty fashion
Goes life: for royal seasons are begun.
Now each new day and each new promise add
    Fresh cause of being glad,
      With vernal passion.

Few leaves upon the branches dare the spring:
    But many buds are making ready,
Trusting the sun, their perfect summer king.
Likewise we put away our wintry cares:
    We hear but happy airs;
        Our hopes are steady.

Cold were the crystal rivers, bitter cold;
    And snows upon the iron mountains;
And withering leaves upon the trodden mould.
Hark to the crystal voices of the rills,
    Falling among the hills,
        From secret fountains!

Long not for June with roses: nor for nights
    Loud with tumultuary thunder:
Those hours wax heavy with their fierce delights.
But April is all bright, and gives us first,
    Before the roses burst,
        Her joy and wonder.

Clear lie the fields, and fade into blue air:
    Here, sweet concerted birds are singing
Around this lawn of sweet grass, warm and fair.
And holy music, through the waving trees,
    Comes gently down the breeze,
        Where bells are ringing.

A Proselyte

    Heart of magnificent desire:
    O equal of the lordly sun!
    Since thou hast cast on me thy fire,
    My cloistral peace, so hardly won,
        Breaks from its trance:
            One glance
    From thee hath all its joy undone.

Of lonely quiet was my dream;
Day gliding into fellow day,
With the mere motion of a stream:
But now in vehement disarray
    Go time and thought,
      Distraught
With passion kindled at thy ray.

Heart of tumultuary might,
O greater than the mountain flame,
That leaps upon the fearful night!
On me thy devastation came,
    Sudden and swift;
      A gift
Of joyous torment without name.

Thy spirit stings my spirit: thou
Takest by storm and ecstasy
The cloister of my soul. And now,
With ardour that is agony,
    I do thy will;
      Yet still
Hear voices of calm memory.

Experience

To George Arthur Greene

The burden of the long gone years: the weight,
The lifeless weight, of miserable things
Done long ago, not done with: the live stings
Left by old joys, follies provoking fate,
Showing their sad side, when it is too late:
Dread burden, that remorseless knowledge brings
To men, remorseful! But the burden clings:
And that remorse declares that bitter state.

113

Wisdom of ages! Wisdom of old age!
Written, and spoken of, and prophesied,
The common record of humanity!
Oh, vain! The springtime is our heritage
First, and the sunlight on the flowing tide:
Then, that old truth's confirming misery.

From *Ireland, with Other Poems*

Oxford

To Arthur Galton

Over, the four long years! And now there rings
One voice of freedom and regret: *Farewell!*
Now old remembrance sorrows, and now sings:
But song from sorrow, now, I cannot tell.

City of weathered cloister and worn court;
Gray city of strong towers and clustering spires:
Where art's fresh loveliness would first resort;
Where lingering art kindled her latest fires.

Where on all hands, wondrous with ancient grace,
Grace touched with age, rise works of goodliest men:
Next Wykeham's art obtain their splendid place
The zeal of Inigo, the strength of Wren.

Where at each coign of every antique street,
A memory hath taken root in stone:
There, Raleigh shone; there, toiled Franciscan feet;
There, Johnson flinched not, but endured, alone.

There, Shelley dreamed his white Platonic dreams;
There, classic Landor throve on Roman thought;
There, Addison pursued his quiet themes;
There, smiled Erasmus, and there, Colet taught.

And there, O memory more sweet than all!
Lived he, whose eyes keep yet our passing light;
Whose crystal lips Athenian speech recall;
Who wears Rome's purple with least pride, most right.

That is the Oxford, strong to charm us yet:
Eternal in her beauty and her past.
What, though her soul be vexed? She can forget
Cares of an hour: only the great things last.

Only the gracious air, only the charm,
And ancient might of true humanities:
These, nor assault of man, nor time, can harm;
Not these, nor Oxford with her memories.

Together have we walked with willing feet
Gardens of plenteous trees, bowering soft lawn:
Hills, whither Arnold wandered; and all sweet
June meadows, from the troubling world withdrawn:

Chapels of cedarn fragrance, and rich gloom
Poured from empurpled panes on either hand:
Cool pavements, carved with legends of the tomb;
Grave haunts, where we might dream, and understand.

Over, the four long years! And unknown powers
Call to us, going forth upon our way:
Ah! turn we, and look back upon the towers,
That rose above our lives, and cheered the day.

Proud and serene, against the sky, they gleam:
Proud and secure, upon the earth, they stand:
Our city hath the air of a pure dream,
And hers indeed is an Hesperian land.

Think of her so! the wonderful, the fair,
The immemorial, and the ever young:
The city, sweet with our forefathers' care;
The city, where the Muses all have sung.

Ill times may be; she hath no thought of time:
She reigns beside the waters yet in pride.
Rude voices cry: but in her ears the chime
Of full, sad bells brings back her old springtide.

Like to a queen in pride of place, she wears
The splendour of a crown in Radcliffe's dome.
Well fare she, well! As perfect beauty fares;
And those high places, that are beauty's home.

from Christmas

II

The last week before Christmas,
    Hoar lies the orchard grass
From pear tree unto apple tree,
    Where feet well shod must pass:
By dripping trees a woodman's fire
    Burns the last leaves, alas!
And the blue smoke drifts through the air,
    Above the branches bare.

The last week before Christmas,
    The last before the snow:
Stand steaming cattle by the hedge,
    With meek heads bending low:
The chattering rivulet flows fast,
    While there is time to flow:
And the blue smoke drifts through the air,
    Above the branches bare.

The last week before Christmas,
    Red berries few to find:
The brown fir cones upon the bough
    Move to a gentle wind:
Down the gray sky go chilly gleams,
    Bringing the sun to mind:
And the blue smoke drifts through the air,
    Above the branches bare.

Oh! last week before Christmas,
    Second before New Year:
Heap heart of oak upon the hearth,
    And keep you now good cheer:
With *Christus natus* for an health,
    And *Christi Mater* dear:
Then blue's the sky, and bright's the air,
    Above the blossoms fair!

Cromwell

To E. K. Chambers

Now, on his last of ways,
    The great September star,
That crowned him on the days
    Of Worcester and Dunbar,
    Shines through the menacing night afar.

This day, his England knows
    Freedom and fear in one;
She holds her breath, while goes
    Her mighty mastering son:
    His sceptre-sword its work hath done.

O crowning mercy, Death!
    Peace to the stormy heart,
Peace to the passionate breath,
    And awful eyes: their part
    Is done, for thou their victor art!

Yet, is it peace with him?
    Answer, O Drogheda's dead!
O ghosts, beside the dim
    Waters and shadows dread!
    What of his coming shall be said?

117

Answer, O fatal King!
   Whose sad, prophetic eyes
Foresaw his glory bring
   Thy death! He also lies
   Dead: hath he peace, O King of sighs?

His soul's most secret thought,
   Eternal Light declares:
He, who in darkness wrought,
   To very Truth now bares
   All hidden hopes, all deep despairs.

Maintains he in Death's land
   The quarrel of the Lord,
As when from his live hand
   Leaped lightnings of the sword?
   Is *Come, good servant!* his reward?

Hath the word come, *Well done!*
   Or the pure word of doom,
Sending him from the sun
   To walk in bitter gloom,
   With the lost angels of the tomb?

Prince of the iron rod
   And war's imperious mail,
Did he indeed for God
   Fight ever, and prevail,
   Bidding the Lord of hosts *All Hail*?

Or was it ardent lust
   Of majesty and might,
That stung and fired and thrust
   His soul into the fight:
   Mystic desire and fierce delight?

Nay, peace for ever more!
　　O martyred souls! He comes,
Your conquered conqueror:
　　No tramplings now, nor drums,
　　Are his, who wrought your martyrdoms.

Tragic, triumphant form,
　　He comes to your dim ways,
Comes upon wings of storm:
　　Greet him, with pardoning praise,
　　With marvelling awe, with equal gaze!

A Stranger

To Will Rothenstein

Her face was like sad things: was like the lights
Of a great city, seen from far off fields,
Or seen from sea: sad things, as are the fires
Lit in a land of furnaces by night:
Sad things, as are the reaches of a stream
Flowing beneath a golden moon alone.
And her clear voice, full of remembrances,
Came like faint music down the distant air.
As though she had a spirit of dead joy
About her, looked the sorrow of her ways:
If light there be, the dark hills are to climb
First: and if calm, far over the long sea.
Fallen from all the world apart she seemed,
Into a silence and a memory.
What had the thin hands done, that now they strained
Together in such passion? And those eyes,
What saw they long ago, that now they dreamed
Along the busy streets, blind but to dreams?
Her white lips mocked the world, and all therein:
She had known more than this; she wanted not
This, who had known the past so great a thing.

Moving about our ways, herself she moved
In things done, years remembered, places gone.
Lonely, amid the living crowds, as dead,
She walked with wonderful and sad regard:
With us, her passing image: but herself
Far over the dark hills and the long sea.

Vinum Dæmonum

To Stephen Phillips

The crystal flame, the ruby flame,
Alluring, dancing, revelling!
See them: and ask me not, whence came
    This cup I bring.

But only watch the wild wine glow,
But only taste its fragrance: then,
Drink the wild drink I bring, and so
    Reign among men.

Only one sting, and then but joy:
One pang of fire, and thou art free.
Then, what thou wilt, thou canst destroy:
    Save only me!

Triumph in tumult of thy lust:
Wanton in passion of thy will:
Cry *Peace!* to conscience, and it must
    At last be still.

I am the Prince of this World: I
Command the flames, command the fires.
Mine are the draughts, that satisfy
    This World's desires.

Thy longing leans across the brink:
Ah, the brave thirst within thine eyes!
For there is that within this drink,
      Which never dies.

Nihilism

To Samuel Smith

Among immortal things not made with hands;
Among immortal things, dead hands have made:
Under the Heavens, upon the Earth, there stands
Man's life, my life: of life I am afraid.

Where silent things, and unimpassioned things,
Where things of nought, and things decaying, are:
I shall be calm soon, with the calm, death brings.
The skies are gray there, without any star.

Only the rest! the rest! Only the gloom,
Soft and long gloom! The pausing from all thought!
My life, I cannot taste: the eternal tomb
Brings me the peace, which life has never brought.

For all the things I do, and do not well;
All the forced drawings of a mortal breath:
Are as the hollow music of a bell,
That times the slow approach of perfect death.

Counsel

To Edward Warren

    Milky pearls of India
    For the braiding of her hair:
    Spice from swart Arabia
    For the fragrance of her air:
Coil the pure pearls, wake the sweet spells,
      Let lutes and hollow shells
Flatter her, fair, if morn be fair.

Stay, no more! Bring not to her
Golden lore of poetry:
Not on those dark eyes confer
Glories of antiquity.
What wouldest thou? She loves too much,
    To feel the solemn touch
Of Plato's thought, that masters thee.

She hath drunken wizard dew,
Where the secret faeries dance:
She hath watched the sylvan crew,
When the forest take the glance
Of the white moon: and she is thine.
    Could Plato's eyes divine
A soul in her wild countenance?

Victory

To George Moore

Down the white steps, into the night, she came;
Wearing white roses, lit by the full moon:
And white upon the shadowy lawn she stood,
Waiting and watching for the dawn's first flame,
Over the dark and visionary wood.
Down the white steps, into the night, she came;
Wearing white roses, lit by the full moon.

Night died away: and over the deep wood
Widened a rosy cloud, a chilly flame:
The shadowy lawn grew cold, and clear, and white.
Then down she drew against her eyes her hood,
To hide away the inexorable light.
Night died away: and over the deep wood
Widened a rosy cloud, a chilly flame.

Then back she turned, and up the white steps came,
And looked into a room of burning lights.
Still slept her loveless husband his brute sleep,
Beside the comfortless and ashen flame:
Her lover waited, where the wood was deep.
She turned not back: but from the white steps came,
And went into the room of burning lights.

Collins

To C. W. Holgate

Through glades and glooms! Oh, fair! Oh, sad!
The paths of song, that led through these
Thy feet, that once were free and glad
To wander beneath Winton trees!
Now in soft shades of sleep they tread
By ways and waters of the dead.

There tender Otway walks with thee,
And Browne, not strange among the dead:
By solemn sounding waters ye,
By willow vallies, gently led,
Think on old memories of her,
Courtly and cloistral Winchester.

So memory's mingled measure flows,
In shadowy dream and twilight trance:
Past death, to dawn of manhood, goes
Thy spirit's unforgetting glance;
Through glades and glooms! And hails at last
The lovely scenes long past: long past.

Te Martyrum Candidatus

To the Very Rev. John Canon O'Hanlon

Ah, see the fair chivalry come, the companions of Christ!
White Horsemen, who ride on white horses, the Knights of God!
They, for their Lord and their Lover who sacrificed
All, save the sweetness of treading, where He first trod!

These through the darkness of death, the dominion of night,
Swept, and they woke in white places at morning tide:
They saw with their eyes, and sang for joy of the sight,
They saw with their eyes the Eyes of the Crucified.

Now, whithersoever He goeth, with Him they go:
White Horsemen, who ride on white horses, oh fair to see!
They ride, where the Rivers of Paradise flash and flow,
White Horsemen, with Christ their Captain: for ever He!

Doctor Major

To Dr Birkbeck Hill

Why, no, Sir! If a barren rascal cries,
    That he is most in love with pleasing woe,
    'Tis plain, Sir! what to think of him: We know
The dog lies; and the dog, too, knows he lies.
Sir! if he's happy, he will dry his eyes,
    And stroll at *Vauxhall* for an hour or so:
    If he's unhappy, it were best he go
Hang himself straight, nor pester us with sighs.

Enough, Sir! Let us have no more of it:
    Your friend is little better than a Whig.
But you and I, Sir, who are men of wit,
    Laugh at the follies of a canting prig.
    Let those who will, Sir! to such whims submit:
No, Sir! we'll to the *Mitre:* Frank! my wig.

Chalkhill

From his Latin epitaph in the Cloisters of Winchester College

Here lies John Chalkhill: years two score,
A Fellow here, and then, no more!
Long life, of chaste and sober mood,
Of silence and of solitude;
Of plenteous alms, of plenteous prayer,
Of sanctity and inward care:
So lived the Church's early fold,
So saintly anchorites of old.
A little child, he did begin
The Heaven of Heavens by storm to win:
At eighty years he entered in.

From Uncollected Poems 1888–1902

Lambeth Lyric

Some seven score Bishops late at Lambeth sat,
Gray-whiskered and respectable debaters:
Each had on head a well-strung curly hat;
    And each wore gaiters.

And when these prelates at their talk had been
Long time, they made yet longer proclamation,
Saying: 'These creeds are childish! both Nicene,
    And Athanasian.

True, they were written by the Holy Ghost;
So, to re-write them were perhaps a pity.
Refer we their revision to a most
    Select Committee!

In ten years' time we wise Pan Anglicans
Once more around this Anglo Catholic table
Will meet, to prove God's word more weak than man's,
          His truth, less stable.'

So saying homeward the good Fathers go;
Up Mississippi [*sic*] some and some up Niger.
For thine old mantle they have clearly no
          More use, Elijah!

Instead, an apostolic apron girds
Their loins, which ministerial fingers tie on:
And Babylon's songs they sing, new tune and words,
          All over Zion.

The Creeds, the Scriptures, all the Faith of old,
They hack and hew to please each bumptious German,
Windy and vague as mists and clouds that fold
          Tabour and Hermon.

Happy Establishment in this thine hour!
Behold thy bishops to their sees retreating!
'Have at the Faith!' each cries: 'goodbye till our
          Next merry meeting!'

                                        [1888]

Fragment: Gray's Inn

Here be the Gardens loved by Lamb;
Here lived my mighty namesake Sam,
And here the venal Verulam:
Brisk Pepys, dear gossip, had his talks,
Oglings, and airs, in Gray's Inn Walks; . . .

                                        [1895]

In Memory of Hubert Crackanthorpe

Requiescat in Pace
Miserere Jesu!

Ours is the darkness, thine the light:
And yet the haunting thought of thee,
O fair and cordial friend! makes bright
The darkness; and we surely see
Thyself, thy very form and face,
Filled with a fresh perfecting grace.

[1897]

A Decadent's Lyric

Sometimes, in very joy of shame,
Our flesh becomes one living flame:
And she and I
Are no more separate, but the same.

Ardour and agony unite;
Desire, delirium, delight:
And I and she
Faint in the fierce and fevered night.

Her body music is: and ah,
The accords of lute and viola!
When she and I
Play on live limbs love's opera!

Dawn

Dim over London breaks
The inevitable day:
Again to hard work wakes
Her world, or harder play.

Swift to their day-sleep go
The lively dreams of night:
We, to our fill of woe,
Or wonder, or delight.

Far into night shall rage
The warfare of the town;
This daily war we wage,
Victors, or smitten down.

Far into night, oh, far!
Some, with no roof but skies,
Shall meet the morning star
With heavy, hopeless eyes.

Faint over London breaks
The inevitable day:
And weary London takes
Once more her strenuous way.

Sylvan Morfydd

White Morfydd through the woods
Went on a moonlit night:
Never so pure a sight
 As that, as white
White Morfydd in the woods.

White Morfydd through the woods
Moved, as a spirit might:
The cool leaves with delight
 Stirred round the white
White Morfydd in the woods.

White Morfydd through the woods
Went lonely and went bright:
She was those woodlands' light,
 My lost, most white
White Morfydd in the woods.

Gracious God rest him! he who toiled so well
    Secrets of grace to tell
Graciously; as the awed rejoicing priest
    Officiates at the feast,
Knowing, how deep within the liturgies
    Lie hid the mysteries.
Half of a passionately pensive soul
    He showed us, not the whole:
Who loved him best, they best, they only, knew
    The deeps they might not view;
That which was private between God and him;
    To others, justly dim.
Calm Oxford autumns and preluding springs!
    To me your memory brings
Delight upon delight, but chiefest one:
    The thought of Oxford's son,
Who gave me of his welcome and his praise,
    When white were still my days;
Ere death had left life darkling, nor had sent
    Lament upon lament:
Ere sorrow told me, how I loved my lost,
    And bade me base love's cost.
Scholarship's constant saint, he kept her light
    In him divinely white:
With cloistral jealousness of ardour strove
    To guard her sacred grove,
Inviolate by worldly feet, nor paced
    In desecrating haste.
Oh, sweet grove smiling of that wisdom, brought
    From arduous ways of thought;
Oh, golden patience of that travailing soul,
    So hungered for the goal,
And vowed to keep, through subtly vigilant pain,
    From pastime on the plain,
Enamoured of the difficult mountain air
    Up beauty's Hill of Prayer!

Stern is the faith of art, right stern, and he
　　Loved her severity.
Momentous things he prized, gradual and fair,
　　Births of a passionate air:
Some austere setting of an ancient sun,
　　Its midday glories done,
Over a silent melancholy sea
　　In sad serenity:
Some delicate dawning of a new desire,
　　Distilling fragrant fire
On hearts of men prophetically fain
　　To feel earth young again:
Some strange rich passage of the dreaming earth,
　　Fulfilled with warmth and worth.
Ended, is service: yet, albeit farewell
　　Tolls the faint vesper bell,
Patient beneath his Oxford trees and towers
　　He still is gently ours:
Hierarch of the spirit, pure and strong,
　　Worthy Uranian song.
Gracious God keep him: and God grant to me
　　By miracle to see
That unforgettably most gracious friend,
　　In the never-ending end!

[1902]

John Davidson

From *In a Music Hall, and Other Poems*

Selene Eden

My dearest lovers know me not;
I hide my life and soul from sight;
I conquer all whose blood is hot;
   My mystery is my mail of might.

I had a troupe who danced with me;
   I veiled myself from head to foot;
My girls were nude as they dared be;
   They sang a chorus, I was mute.

But now I fill the widest stage
   Alone, unveiled, without a song;
And still with mystery I engage
   The aching senses of the throng.

A dark-blue vest with stars of gold,
   My only diamond in my hair,
An Indian scarf about me rolled;
   That is the dress I always wear.

At first the sensuous music whets
   The lustful crowd; the dim-lit room
Recalls delights, recalls regrets;
   And then I enter in the gloom.

I glide, I trip, I run, I spin,
   Lapped in the lime-light's aureole,
Hushed are the voices, hushed the din,
   I see men's eyes like glowing coal.

My loosened scarf in odours drenched
  Showers keener hints of sensual bliss;
The music swoons, the light is quenched,
  Into the dark I throw a kiss.

Then, like a long wave rolling home,
  The music gathers speed and sound;
I, dancing, am the music's foam,
  And wilder, fleeter, higher bound,

And fling my feet above my head;
  The light grows; none aside may glance;
Crimson and amber, green and red,
  In blinding baths of these I dance.

And soft, and sweet, and calm, my face
  Looks pure as unsunned chastity,
Even in the whirling triple pace:
  That is my conquering mystery.

From *Fleet Street Eclogues*

New Year's Day

BASIL   SANDY   BRIAN

BRIAN
This trade that we ply with the pen,
Unworthy of heroes or men,
Assorts ever less with my humour:
Mere tongues in the raiment of rumour,
We review and report and invent:
In drivel our virtue is spent.

BASIL

From the muted tread of the feet,
And the slackening wheels, I know
The air is hung with snow,
And carpeted the street.

BRIAN

Ambition, and passion, and power
Come out of the north and the west,
Every year, every day, every hour,
Into Fleet Street to fashion their best:
They would shape what is noble and wise;
They must live by a traffic in lies.

BASIL

Sweet rivers of living blood
Poured into an ocean of mud.

BRIAN

Newspapers flap o'er the land,
And darken the face of the sky;
A covey of dragons, wide-vanned,
Circle-wise clanging, they fly.
No nightingale sings; overhead
The lark never mounts to the sun;
Beauty and truth are dead,
And the end of the world begun.

BASIL

Far away in a valley of peace,
Swaddled in emerald,
The snow-happed primroses
Tarry till spring has called.

SANDY

And here where the Fleet once tripped
In its ditch to the drumlie Thames,
We journalists, haughty though hipped,
Are calling our calling names.

BRIAN

But you know, as I know, that our craft
Is the meanest in act and intention;
You know that the Time-spirit laughed
In his sleeve at the Dutchman's invention:
Old Coster of Haarlem, I mean,
Whose print was the first ever seen.

BASIL

I can hear in that valley of mine,
Loud-voiced on a leafless spray,
How the robin sings, flushed with his holly wine,
Of the moonlight blossoms of May.

BRIAN

These dragons that hide the sun!
The serpents flying and fiery,
That knotted a nation in one
Writhen mass: the scaley and wirey,
And flame breathing terror the saint
Still slays on our coins; the thing
That wandering artists paint
Where creaking sign-boards swing;
Gargouille, famous in France
That the fire at Rouen slew;
The dragon, Petrarca's lance
In Laura's defence overthrew;
The sea-beast Perseus killed;
Proserpine's triple team;
Tarasque whose blood was spilled
In Rhone's empurpled stream;
For far-flying strength and ire
And venom might never withstand
The least of the flourishing quire
In Fleet Street stalled and the Strand.

BASIL

Through the opening gate of the year
Sunbeams and snowdrops peer.

BRIAN
Fed by us here and groomed
In this pestilent reeking stye,
These dragons I say have doomed
Religion and poetry.

SANDY
They may doom till the moon forsakes
Her dark, star-daisied lawn;
They may doom till doomsday breaks
With angels to trumpet the dawn;
While love enchants the young,
And the old have sorrow and care,
No song shall be unsung,
Unprayed no prayer.

BRIAN
Leaving the dragons alone –
I say what the prophet says –
The tyrant on the throne
Is the morning and evening press.
In all the land his spies,
A little folk but strong,
A second plague of flies,
Buzz of the right and the wrong;
Swarm in our ears and our eyes –
News and scandal and lies.
Men stand upon the brink
Of a precipice every day;
A drop of printer's ink
Their poise may overweigh;
So they think what the papers think,
And do as the papers say.
Who reads the daily press,
His soul's lost here and now;
Who writes for it is less
Than the beast that tugs a plough.

BASIL

Round happy household fires
I hear sweet voices sing;
And the lamb's-wool of our sires,
Spiced ale, is a draught for a king.

SANDY

Now, journalist, perpend.
You soil your bread and butter:
Shall guttersnipes pretend
To satirize the gutter?
Are parsons ever seen
To butt against the steeple?
Brian, I fear you've been
With very superior people.
We, the valour and brains of the age,
The brilliant, adventurous souls,
No longer in berserkir rage –

BRIAN

Spare us the berserkir rage!

SANDY

Not I; the phrase outrolls
As freshly to me this hour,
As when on my boyish sense
It struck like a trumpet-blare.
You may cringe and cower
To critical pretence;
If people will go bare
They may count on bloody backs;
Cold are the hearts that care
If a girl be blue-eyed or black-eyed;
Only to souls of hacks
Are phrases hackneyed. –
When the damsel had her bower,
And the lady kept her state,
The splendour and the power
That made adventure great,

Were not more strong and splendid
Than the subtle might we wield;
Though chivalry be ended,
There are champions in the field.
Nor are we warriors giftless;
Deep magic's in our stroke;
Ours are the shoes of swiftness:
And ours the darkling cloak;
We fear no golden charmer;
We dread no form of words;
We wear enchanted armour;
We wield enchanted swords.
To us the hour belongs;
Our daily victory is
O'er hydras, giant wrongs,
And dwarf iniquities.
We also may behold,
Before our boys are old,
When time shall have unfurled
His heavy hanging mists,
How the future of the world
Was shaped by journalists.

BASIL
Sing hey for the journalist!
He is your true soldado;
Both time and chance he'll lead a dance,
And find out Eldorado.

BRIAN
Sing hey for Eldorado!

BASIL
A catch, a catch, we'll trowl!

BRIAN
Sing hey for Eldorado!

SANDY
And bring a mazer-bowl,
With ale a-frothing brimmed.

BRIAN
We may not rest without it.

SANDY
With dainty ribbons trimmed,
And love-birds carved about it.

BASIL
With roasted apples scented,
And spiced with cloves and mace.

BRIAN
Praise him who ale invented!

SANDY
In heaven he has a place!

BASIL
Such a camarado
Heaven's hostel never missed!

BRIAN
Sing hey for Eldorado!

SANDY
Sing ho for the journalist!

BASIL
We drink them and we sing them
In mighty humming ale.

BRAIN
May fate together bring them!

SANDY

Amen!

BASIL

       Wass hael!

BRIAN

             Drinc hael!

From *Ballads and Songs*

A Ballad of Heaven

He wrought at one great work for years;
   The world passed by with lofty look:
Sometimes his eyes were dashed with tears;
   Sometimes his lips with laughter shook.

His wife and child went clothed in rags,
   And in a windy garret starved:
He trod his measures on the flags,
   And high on heaven his music carved.

Wistful he grew but never feared;
   For always on the midnight skies
His rich orchestral score appeared
   In stars and zones and galaxies.

He thought to copy down his score:
   The moonlight was his lamp: he said,
'Listen, my love;' but on the floor
   His wife and child were lying dead.

Her hollow eyes were open wide;
   He deemed she heard with special zest:
Her death's-head infant coldly eyed
   The desert of her shrunken breast.

'Listen, my love: my work is done;
    I tremble as I touch the page
To sign the sentence of the sun
    And crown the great eternal age.

'The slow adagio begins;
    The winding-sheets are ravelled out
That swathe the minds of men, the sins
    That wrap their rotting souls about.

'The dead are heralded along;
    With silver trumps and golden drums,
And flutes and oboes, keen and strong,
    My brave andante singing comes.

'Then like a python's sumptuous dress
    The frame of things is cast away,
And out of Time's obscure distress,
    The thundering scherzo crashes Day.

'For three great orchestras I hope
    My mighty music shall be scored:
On three high hills they shall have scope
    With heaven's vault for a sounding-board.

'Sleep well, love; let your eyelids fall;
    Cover the child; goodnight, and if . . .
What? Speak . . . the traitorous end of all!
    Both . . . cold and hungry . . . cold and stiff!

'But no, God means us well, I trust:
    Dear ones, be happy, hope is nigh:
We are too young to fall to dust,
    And too unsatisfied to die.'

He lifted up against his breast
    The woman's body stark and wan;
And to her withered bosom pressed
    The little skin-clad skeleton.

'You see you are alive,' he cried.
　He rocked them gently to and fro.
'No, no, my love, you have not died;
　Nor you, my little fellow; no.'

Long in his arms he strained his dead
　And crooned an antique lullaby;
Then laid them on the lowly bed,
　And broke down with a doleful cry.

'The love, the hope, the blood, the brain,
　Of her and me, the budding life,
And my great music – all in vain!
　My unscored work, my child, my wife!

'We drop into oblivion,
　And nourish some suburban sod:
My work, this woman, this my son,
　Are now no more: there is no God.

'The world's a dustbin; we are due,
　And death's cart waits: be life accurst!'
He stumbled down beside the two,
　And clasping them, his great heart burst.

Straightway he stood at heaven's gate,
　Abashed and trembling for his sin:
I trow he had not long to wait,
　For God came out and led him in.

And then there ran a radiant pair,
　Ruddy with haste and eager-eyed
To meet him first upon the stair –
　His wife and child beatified.

They clad him in a robe of light,
　And gave him heavenly food to eat;
Great seraphs praised him to the height,
　Archangels sat about his feet.

God, smiling, took him by the hand,
    And led him to the brink of heaven:
He saw where systems whirling stand,
    Where galaxies like snow are driven.

Dead silence reigned; a shudder ran
    Through space; Time furled his wearied wings;
A slow adagio then began
    Sweetly resolving troubled things.

The dead were heralded along:
    As if with drums and trumps of flame,
And flutes and oboes keen and strong,
    A brave andante singing came.

Then like a python's sumptuous dress
    The frame of things was cast away,
And out of Time's obscure distress
    The conquering scherzo thundered Day.

He doubted; but God said 'Even so;
    Nothing is lost that's wrought with tears:
The music that you made below
    Is now the music of the spheres.'

London

Athwart the sky a lowly sigh
    From west to east the sweet wind carried;
The sun stood still on Primrose Hill;
    His light in all the city tarried:
The clouds on viewless columns bloomed
Like smouldering lilies unconsumed.

Oh sweetheart, see! how shadowy,
  Of some occult magician's rearing,
Or swung in space of heaven's grace
  Dissolving, dimly reappearing,
Afloat upon ethereal tides
St Paul's above the city rides!

A rumour broke through the thin smoke
  Enwreathing abbey, tower, and palace,
The parks, the squares, the thoroughfares,
  The million-peopled lanes and alleys,
An ever-muttering prisoned storm,
The heart of London beating warm.

In Romney Marsh

As I went down to Dymchurch Wall,
  I heard the South sing o'er the land;
I saw the yellow sunlight fall
  On knolls where Norman churches stand.

And ringing shrilly, taut and lithe,
  Within the wind a core of sound,
The wire from Romney town to Hythe
  Alone its airy journey wound.

A veil of purple vapour flowed
  And trailed its fringe along the Straits;
The upper air like sapphire glowed;
  And roses filled Heaven's central gates.

Masts in the offing wagged their tops;
  The swinging waves pealed on the shore;
The saffron beach, all diamond drops
  And beads of surge, prolonged the roar.

As I came up from Dymchurch Wall,
    I saw above the Downs' low crest
The crimson brands of sunset fall,
    Flicker and fade from out the west.

Night sank: like flakes of silver fire
    The stars in one great shower came down;
Shrill blew the wind; and shrill the wire
    Rang out from Hythe to Romney town.

The darkly shining salt sea drops
    Streamed as the waves clashed on the shore;
The beach, with all its organ stops
    Pealing again, prolonged the roar.

Thirty Bob a Week

I couldn't touch a stop and turn a screw,
    And set the blooming world a-work for me,
Like such as cut their teeth – I hope, like you –
    On the handle of a skeleton gold key;
I cut mine on a leek, which I eat it every week:
    I'm a clerk at thirty bob as you can see.

But I don't allow it's luck and all a toss;
    There's no such thing as being starred and crossed;
It's just the power of some to be a boss,
    And the bally power of others to be bossed:
I face the music, sir; you bet I ain't a cur;
    Strike me lucky if I don't believe I'm lost!

For like a mole I journey in the dark,
    A-travelling along the underground
From my Pillar'd Halls and broad Suburbean Park,
    To come the daily dull official round;
And home again at night with my pipe all alight,
    A-scheming how to count ten bob a pound.

And it's often very cold and very wet,
  And my missis stitches towels for a hunks;
And the Pillar'd Halls is half of it to let –
  Three rooms about the size of travelling trunks.
And we cough, my wife and I, to dislocate a sigh,
  When the noisy little kids are in their bunks.

But you never hear her do a growl or whine,
  For she's made of flint and roses, very odd;
And I've got to cut my meaning rather fine,
  Or I'd blubber, for I'm made of greens and sod:
So p'r'aps we are in Hell for all that I can tell,
  And lost and damn'd and served up hot to God.

I ain't blaspheming, Mr Silver-tongue;
  I'm saying things a bit beyond your art:
Of all the rummy starts you ever sprung,
  Thirty bob a week's the rummiest start!
With your science and your books and your the'ries about spooks,
  Did you ever hear of looking in your heart?

I didn't mean your pocket, Mr, no:
  I mean that having children and a wife,
With thirty bob on which to come and go,
  Isn't dancing to the tabor and the fife:
When it doesn't make you drink, by Heaven! it makes you think,
  And notice curious items about life.

I step into my heart and there I meet
  A god-almighty devil singing small,
Who would like to shout and whistle in the street,
  And squelch the passers flat against the wall;
If the whole world was a cake he had the power to take,
  He would take it, ask for more, and eat it all.

And I meet a sort of simpleton beside,
  The kind that life is always giving beans;
With thirty bob a week to keep a bride
  He fell in love and married in his teens:
At thirty bob he stuck; but he knows it isn't luck:
  He knows the seas are deeper than tureens.

And the god-almighty devil and the fool
  That meet me in the High Street on the strike,
When I walk about my heart a-gathering wool,
  Are my good and evil angels if you like.
And both of them together in every kind of weather
  Ride me like a double-seated bike.

That's rough a bit and needs its meaning curled.
  But I have a high old hot un in my mind –
A most engrugious notion of the world,
  That leaves your lightning 'rithmetic behind
I give it at a glance when I say 'There ain't no chance,
  Nor nothing of the lucky-lottery kind.'

And it's this way that I make it out to be:
  No fathers, mothers, countries, climates – none;
Not Adam was responsible for me,
  Nor society, nor systems, nary one:
A little sleeping seed, I woke – I did, indeed –
  A million years before the blooming sun.

I woke because I thought the time had come;
  Beyond my will there was no other cause;
And everywhere I found myself at home,
  Because I chose to be the thing I was;
And in whatever shape of mollusc or of ape
  I always went according to the laws.

I was the love that chose my mother out;
    I joined two lives and from the union burst;
My weakness and my strength without a doubt
    Are mine alone for ever from the first:
It's just the very same with a difference in the name
    As 'Thy will be done.' You say it if you durst!

They say it daily up and down the land
    As easy as you take a drink, it's true;
But the difficultest go to understand,
    And the difficultest job a man can do,
Is to come it brave and meek with thirty bob a week,
    And feel that that's the proper thing for you.

It's a naked child against a hungry wolf;
    It's playing bowls upon a splitting wreck;
It's walking on a string across a gulf
    With millstones fore-and-aft about your neck;
But the thing is daily done by many and many a one;
    And we fall, face forward, fighting, on the deck.

A Cinque Port

Below the down the stranded town,
    What may betide forlornly waits,
With memories of smoky skies,
    When Gallic navies crossed the straits;
When waves with fire and blood grew bright.
And cannon thundered through the night.

With swinging stride the rhythmic tide
    Bore to the harbour barque and sloop;
Across the bar the ship of war,
    In castled stern and lanterned poop,
Came up with conquests on her lee,
The stately mistress of the sea.

Where argosies have wooed the breeze,
   The simple sheep are feeding now;
And near and far across the bar
   The ploughman whistles at the plough;
Where once the long waves washed the shore,
Larks from their lowly lodgings soar.

Below the down the stranded town
   Hears far away the rollers beat;
About the wall the seabirds call;
   The salt wind murmurs through the street;
Forlorn the sea's forsaken bride,
Awaits the end that shall betide.

from A Loafer

I hang about the streets all day,
   At night I hang about;
I sleep a little when I may,
   But rise betimes the morning's scout;
For through the year I always hear
   Afar, aloft, a ghostly shout.

My clothes are worn to threads and loops;
   My skin shows here and there;
About my face like seaweed droops
   My tangled beard, my tangled hair;
From cavernous and shaggy brows
   My stony eyes untroubled stare.

I move from eastern wretchedness
   Through Fleet Street and the Strand;
And as the pleasant people press
   I touch them softly with my hand,
Perhaps to know that still I go
   Alive about a living land.

For, far in front the clouds are riven;
    I hear the ghostly cry,
As if a still voice fell from heaven
    To where sea-whelmed the drowned folk lie
In sepulchres no tempest stirs
    And only eyeless things pass by.

In Piccadilly spirits pass:
    Oh, eyes and cheeks that glow!
Oh, strength and comeliness! Alas,
    The lustrous health is earth I know
From shrinking eyes that recognize
    No brother in my rags and woe.

I know no handicraft, no art,
    But I have conquered fate;
For I have chosen the better part,
    And neither hope, nor fear, nor hate.
With placid breath on pain and death,
    My certain alms, alone I wait.

And daily, nightly comes the call,
    The pale, unechoing note,
The faint 'Aha!' sent from the wall
    Of heaven, but from no ruddy throat
Of human breed or seraph's seed,
    A phantom voice that cries by rote.

From *New Ballads*

A Woman and Her Son

'Has he come yet?' the dying woman asked.
'No,' said the nurse. 'Be quiet.'
                        'When he comes
Bring him to me: I may not live an hour.'
'Not if you talk. Be quiet.'
                        'When he comes
Bring him to me.'

'Hush, will you!'

Night came down.
The cries of children playing in the street
Suddenly rose more voluble and shrill;
Ceased, and broke out again: and ceased and broke
In eager prate; then dwindled and expired.

'Across the dreary common once I saw
The moon rise out of London like a ghost.
Has the moon risen? Is he come?'

'Not yet.
Be still, or you will die before he comes.'

The working-men with heavy iron tread,
The thin-shod clerks, the shopmen neat and plump
Home from the city came. On muddy beer
The melancholy mean suburban street
Grew maudlin for an hour; pianos waked
In dissonance from dreams of rusty peace,
And unpitched voices quavered tedious songs
Of sentiment infirm or nerveless mirth.

'Has he come yet?'
'Be still or you will die!'

And when the hour of gaiety had passed,
And the poor revellers were gone to bed,
The moon among the chimneys wandering long
Escaped at last, and sadly overlooked
The waste raw land where doleful suburbs thrive.

Then came a firm quick step – measured but quick;
And then a triple knock that shook the house
And brought the plaster down.

                         'My son!' she cried.
'Bring him to me!'

                    He came; the nurse went out.

'Mother, I thought to spare myself this pain.'
He said at once, 'but that was cowardly.
And so I come to bid you try to think,
To understand at last.'

                  'Still hard, my son?'
'Hard as the nether millstone.'

                  'But I hope
To soften you,' she said, 'before I die.'

'And I to see you harden with a hiss
As life goes out in the cold bath of death.
Oh, surely now your creed will set you free
For one great moment, and the universe
Flash on your intellect as power, power, power,
Knowing not good or evil, God or sin,
But only everlasting yea and nay.
Is weakness greatness? No, a thousand times!
Is force the greatest? Yes, for ever yes!
Be strong, be great, now you have come to die.'

'My son, you seem to me a kind of prig.'

'How can I get it said? Think, mother, think!
Look back upon your fifty wretched years
And show me anywhere the hand of God.
Your husband saving souls – O, paltry souls
That need salvation! – lost the grip of things,
And left you penniless with none to aid
But me the prodigal. Back to the start!
An orphan girl, hurt, melancholy, frail,
Before you learned to play, your toil began:

151

That might have been your making, had the weight
Of drudgery, the unsheathed fire of woe
Borne down and beat on your defenceless life:
Souls shrivel up in these extremes of pain,
Or issue diamonds to engrave the world;
But yours before it could be made or marred,
Plucked from the burning, saved by faith, became
Inferior as a thing of paste that hopes
To pass for real in heaven's enduring* light.
You married then a crude evangelist,
Whose soul was like a wafer that can take
One single impress only.'

       'Oh, my son!
Your father!'

       'He, my father! These are times
When all must to the crucible – no thought,
Practice, or use, or custom sacro-sanct
But shall be violable now. And first
If ever we evade the wonted round,
The stagnant vortex of the eddying years,
The child must take the father by the beard,
And say, "What did you in begetting me?"'

'I will not listen!'

       'But you shall, you must –
You cannot help yourself. Death in your eyes
And voice, and I to torture you with truth,
Even as your preachers for a thousand years
Pestered with falsehood souls of dying folk.
Look at the man, your husband. Of the soil;
Broad, strong, adust; head, massive; eyes of steel;
Yet some way ailing, for he understood
But one idea, and he married you.'

* 'In Davidson's text the word "enduing" is presumably a misprint' –
Maurice Lindsay.

The dying woman sat up straight in bed;
A ghastly blush glowed on her yellow cheek,
And flame broke from her her eyes, but words came not.

The son's pent wrath burnt on. 'He married you;
You were his wife, his servant; cheerfully
You bore him children; and your house was hell.
Unwell, half-starved, and clad in cast-off clothes,
We had no room, no sport; nothing but fear
Of our evangelist, whose little purse
Opened to all save us; who squandered smiles
On wily proselytes, and gloomed at home.
You had eight children; only three grew up;
Of these, one died bedrid, and one insane,
And I alone am left you. Think of it!
It matters nothing if a fish, a plant
Teem with waste offspring, but a conscious womb!
Eight times you bore a child, and in fierce throes,
For you were frail and small: of all your love,
Your hopes, your passion, not a memory steals
To smooth your dying pillow, only I
Am here to rack you. Where does God appear?'

'God shall appear,' the dying woman said.
'God has appeared: my heart is in his hand.
Were there no God, no Heaven! – Oh, foolish boy!
You foolish fellow! Pain and trouble here
Are God's benignest providence – the whip
And spur to Heaven. But joy was mine below –
I am unjust to God – great joy was mine:
Which makes Heaven sweeter too; because if earth
Afford such pleasure in mortality
What must immortal happiness be like!
Eight times I was a mother. Frail and small?
Yes; but the passionate, courageous mate
Of a strong man. Oh, boy! You paltry boy!
Hush! Think! Think – you! Eight times I bore a child,

Eight souls for God! In Heaven they wait for me –
My husband and the seven. I see them all!
And two are children still – my little ones!
While I have sorrowed here, shrinking sometimes
From that which was decreed, my Father, God,
Was storing Heaven with treasure for me. Hush!
My dowry in the skies! God's thoughtfulness!
I see it all! Lest Heaven might, unalloyed,
Distress my shy soul, I leave earth in doubt
Of your salvation: something to hope and fear
Until I get accustomed to the peace
That passeth understanding. When you come –
For you will come, my son. . . .'

                              Her strength gave out;
She sank down panting, bathed in tears and sweat.

'Could I but touch your intellect,' he cried,
'Before you die! Mother, the world is mad:
This castle in the air, this Heaven of yours,
Is the lewd dream of morbid vanity.
For each of us death is the end of all;
And when the sun goes out the race of men
Shall cease for ever. It is ours to make
This farce of fate a splendid tragedy:
Since we must be the sport of circumstance,
We should be sportsmen, and produce a breed
Of gallant creatures, conscious of their doom,
Marching with lofty brows, game to the last.
Oh good and evil, heaven and hell are lies!
But strength is great: there is no other truth:
This is the yea-and-nay that makes men hard.
Mother, be hard and happy in your death.'

'What do you say? I hear the waters roll . . .'
Then, with a faint cry, striving to arise –
'After I die I shall come back to you,
And then you must believe; you must believe,
For I shall bring you news of God and Heaven!'

He set his teeth, and saw his mother die.
Outside a city-reveller's tipsy tread
Severed the silence with a jagged rent;
The tall lamps flickered through the sombre street,
With yellow light hiding the stainless stars:
In the next house a child awoke and cried;
Far off a clank and clash of shunting trains
Broke out and ceased, as if the fettered world
Started and shook its irons in the night;
Across the dreary common citywards,
The moon, among the chimneys sunk again,
Cast on the clouds a shade of smoky pearl.

And when her funeral day had come, her son,
Before they fastened down the coffin lid,
Shut himself in the chamber, there to gaze
Upon her dead face, hardening his heart.
But as he gazed, into the smooth wan cheek
Life with its wrinkles shot again; the eyes
Burst open, and the bony fingers clutched
The coffin sides; the woman raised herself,
And owl-like in her shroud blinked on the light.
'Mother, what news of God and Heaven?' he asked.
Feeble and strange, her voice came from afar:
'I am not dead: I must have been asleep.'

'Do not imagine that. You lay here dead –
Three days and nights, a corpse. Life has come back:
Often it does, although faint-hearted folk
Fear to admit it: none of those who die,
And come to life again, can ever tell
Of any bourne from which they have returned:
Therefore they were not dead, your casuists say.
The ancient jugglery that tricks the world!
You lay here dead, three days and nights. What news?
"After I die I shall come back to you,
And then you must believe" – these were your words –
"For I shall bring you news of God and Heaven."'

She cast a look forlorn about the room:
The door was shut; the worn venetian, down;
And stuffy sunlight through the dusty slats
Spotted the floor, and smeared the faded walls.
He with his strident voice and eyes of steel
Stood by relentless.

                  'I remember, dear,'
She whispered, 'very little. When I died
I saw my children dimly bending down,
The little ones in front, to beckon me,
A moment in the dark; and that is all.'

'That was before you died – the last attempt
Of fancy to create the heart's desire.
Now mother, be courageous; now, be hard.'

'What must I say or do, my dearest son?
Oh me, the deep discomfort of my mind!
Come to me, hold me, help me to be brave,
And I shall make you happy if I can,
For I have none but you – none anywhere . . .
Mary, the youngest, whom you never saw
Looked out of Heaven first: her little hands . . .
Three days and nights, dead, and no memory! . . .
A poor old creature dying a second death,
I understand the settled treachery,
The plot of love and hope against the world.
Fearless, I gave myself at nature's call;
And when they died, my children, one by one,
All sweetly in my heart I buried them.
Who stole them while I slept? Where are they all?
My heart is eerie, like a rifled grave
Where silent spiders spin among the dust,
And the wind moans and laughs under its breath.
But in a drawer. . . . What is there in the drawer?

No pressure of a little rosy hand
Upon a faded cheek – nor anywhere
The seven fair stars I made. Oh love the cheat!
And hope, the radiant devil pointing up,
Lest men should cease to give the couple sport
And end the world at once! For three days dead –
Here in my coffin; and no memory!
Oh, it is hard! But I – I, too, am hard . . .
Be hard, my son, and steep your heart of flesh
In stony waters till it grows a stone,
Or love and hope will hack it with blunt knives
As long as it can feel.'

              He, holding her,
With sobs and laughter spoke: his mind had snapped
Like a frayed string o'erstretched: 'Mother, rejoice;
For I shall make you glad. There is no heaven.
Your children are resolved to dust and dew:
But, mother, I am God. I shall create
The heaven of your desires. There must be heaven
For mothers and their babes. Let heaven be now!'
They found him conjuring chaos with mad words
And brandished hands across his mother's corpse.

Thus did he see her harden with a hiss
As life went out in the cold bath of death;
Thus did she soften him before she died:
For both were bigots – fateful souls that plague
The gentle world.

Piper, Play!

Now the furnaces are out,
    And the aching anvils sleep;
Down the road the grimy rout
    Tramples homeward twenty deep.

Piper, play! Piper, play!
　　Though we be o'erlaboured men,
　Ripe for rest, pipe your best!
　　Let us foot it once again!

Bridled looms delay their din;
　All the humming wheels are spent;
Busy spindles cease to spin;
　Warp and woof must rest content.
　　Piper, play! Piper, play!
　　　For a little we are free!
　　Foot it girls and shake your curls,
　　　　Haggard creatures though we be!

Racked and soiled the faded air
　Freshens in our holiday;
Clouds and tides our respite share;
　Breezes linger by the way.
　　Piper, rest! Piper, rest!
　　　Now, a carol of the moon!
　　Piper, piper, play your best!
　　　Melt the sun into your tune!

We are of the humblest grade;
　Yet we dare to dance our fill:
Male and female were we made –
　Fathers, mothers, lovers still!
　　Piper – softly; soft and low;
　　　Pipe of love in mellow notes,
　　Till the tears begin to flow,
　　　And our hearts are in our throats!

Nameless as the stars of night
　Far in galaxies unfurled,
Yet we wield unrivalled might,
　Joints and hinges of the world!

Night and day! night and day!
  Sound the song the hours rehearse!
Work and play! work and play!
  The order of the universe!

Now the furnaces are out,
  And the aching anvils sleep;
Down the road a merry rout
  Dances homeward, twenty deep.
    Piper, play! Piper, play!
      Wearied people though we be,
    Ripe for rest, pipe your best!
      For a little we are free!

A Northern Suburb

Nature selects the longest way,
  And winds about in tortuous grooves;
A thousand years the oaks decay;
  The wrinkled glacier hardly moves.

But here the whetted fangs of change
  Daily devour the old demesne –
The busy farm, the quiet grange,
  The wayside inn, the village green.

In gaudy yellow brick and red,
  With rooting pipes, like creepers rank,
The shoddy terraces o'erspread
  Meadow, and garth, and daisied bank.

With shelves for rooms the houses crowd,
  Like draughty cupboards in a row –
Ice-chests when wintry winds are loud,
  Ovens when summer breezes blow.

Roused by the fee'd policeman's knock,
   And sad that day should come again,
Under the stars the workmen flock
   In haste to reach the workmen's train.

For here dwell those who must fulfil
   Dull tasks in uncongenial spheres,
Who toil through dread of coming ill,
   And not with hope of happier years –

The lowly folk who scarcely dare
   Conceive themselves perhaps misplaced,
Whose prize for unremitting care
   Is only not to be disgraced.

From *The Last Ballad and Other Poems*

Insomnia

He wakened quivering on a golden rack
   Inlaid with gems: no sign of change, no fear
   Or hope of death came near;
Only the empty ether hovered black
   About him stretched upon his living bier,
Of old by Merlin's Master deftly wrought:
   Two Seraphim of Gabriel's helpful race
   In that far nook of space
With iron levers wrenched and held him taut.

The Seraph at his head was Agony;
   Delight, more terrible, stood at his feet:
   Their sixfold pinions beat
The darkness, or were spread immovably,
   Poising the rack, whose jewelled fabric meet
To strain a god, did fitfully unmask
   With olive light of chrysoprases dim
   The smiling Seraphim
Implacably intent upon their task.

In the Isle of Dogs

While the water-wagon's ringing showers
Sweetened the dust with a woodland smell,
'Past noon, past noon, two sultry hours,'
Drowsily fell
From the schoolhouse clock
In the Isle of Dogs by Millwall Dock.

Mirrored in shadowy windows draped
With ragged net or half-drawn blind
Bowsprits, masts, exactly shaped
To woo or fight the wind,
Like monitors of guilt
By strength and beauty sent,
Disgraced the shameful houses built
To furnish rent.

From the pavements and the roofs
In shimmering volumes wound
The wrinkled heat;
Distant hammers, wheels and hoofs,
A turbulent pulse of sound,
Southward obscurely beat,
The only utterance of the afternoon,
Till on a sudden in the silent street
An organ-man drew up and ground
The Old Hundredth tune.

Forthwith the pillar of cloud that hides the past
Burst into flame,
Whose alchemy transmuted house and mast,
Street, dockyard, pier and pile:
By magic sound the Isle of Dogs became
A northern isle –
A green isle like a beryl set
In a wine-coloured sea,
Shadowed by mountains where a river met
The ocean's arm extended royally.

There also in the evening on the shore
An old man ground the Old Hundredth tune,
An old enchanter steeped in human lore,
Sad-eyed, with whitening beard, and visage lank:
Not since and not before,
Under the sunset or the mellowing moon,
Has any hand of man's conveyed
Such meaning in the turning of a crank.

Sometimes he played
As if his box had been
An organ in an abbey richly lit;
For when the dark invaded day's demesne,
And the sun set in crimson and in gold;
When idlers swarmed upon the esplanade,
And a late steamer wheeling towards the quay
Struck founts of silver from the darkling sea,
The solemn tune arose and shook and rolled
Above the throng,
Above the hum and tramp and bravely knit
All hearts in common memories of song.

Sometimes he played at speed;
Then the Old Hundredth like a devil's mass
Instinct with evil thought and evil deed,
Rang out in anguish and remorse. Alas!
That men must know both Heaven and Hell!
Sometimes the melody
Sang with the murmuring surge;
And with the winds would tell
Of peaceful graves and of the passing bell.
Sometimes it pealed across the bay
A high triumphal dirge,
A dirge
For the departing undefeated day.

A noble tune, a high becoming mate
Of the capped mountains and the deep broad firth;
A simple tune and great,
The fittest utterance of the voice of earth.

Romance

THE MERCHANTMAN   THE MARKETHAUNTERS

THE MARKETHAUNTERS
Now, while our money is piping hot
    From the mint of our toil that coins the sheaves,
Merchantman, merchantman, what have you got
    In your tabernacle hung with leaves?
        What have you got?
            The sun rides high;
        Our money is hot;
            We must buy, buy, buy!

THE MERCHANTMAN
I come from the elfin king's demesne
    With chrysolite, hyacinth, tourmaline;
I have emeralds here of living green;
    I have rubies, each like a cup of wine;
And diamonds, diamonds that never have been
    Outshone by eyes the most divine!

THE MARKETHAUNTERS
Jewellery? – Baubles; bad for the soul;
    Desire of the heart and lust of the eye!
Diamonds, indeed! We wanted coal.
    What else do you sell? Come, sound your cry!
        Our money is hot;
            The night draws nigh;
        What have you got
            That we want to buy?

163

THE MERCHANTMAN

I have here enshrined the soul of the rose
    Exhaled in the land of the daystar's birth;
I have casks whose golden staves enclose
    Eternal youth, eternal mirth;
And cordials that bring repose,
    And the tranquil night, and the end of the earth.

THE MARKETHAUNTERS

Rapture of wine? But it never pays:
    We must keep our common sense alert.
Raisins are healthier, medicine says –
    Raisins and almonds for dessert.
        But we want to buy;
           For our money is hot,
        And age draws nigh:
           What else have you got?

THE MERCHANTMAN

I have lamps that gild the lustre of noon;
    Shadowy arrows that pierce the brain;
Dulcimers strung with beams of the moon;
    Psalteries fashioned of pleasure and pain;
A song and a sword and a haunting tune
    That may never be offered the world again.

THE MARKETHAUNTERS

Dulcimers! psalteries! Whom do you mock?
    Arrows and songs? We have axes to grind!
Shut up your booth and your mouldering stock,
    For we never shall deal. – Come away; let us find
        What the others have got
           We must buy, buy, buy;
        For our money is hot,
           And death draws nigh.

Holiday at Hampton Court

Scales of pearly cloud inlay
   North and south the turquoise sky,
While the diamond lamp of day
   Quenchless burns, and time on high
A moment halts upon his way
   Bidding noon again good-bye.

Gaffers, gammers, huzzies, louts,
   Couples, gangs, and families
Sprawling, shake, with Babel-shouts
   Bluff King Hal's funereal trees;
And eddying groups of stare-abouts
   Quiz the sandstone Hercules.

When their tongues and tempers tire,
   Harry and his little lot
Condescendingly admire
   Lozenge-bed and crescent-plot,
Aglow with links of azure fire,
   Pansy and forget-me-not.

Where the emerald shadows rest
   In the lofty woodland aisle,
Chaffing lovers quaintly dressed
   Chase and double many a mile,
Indifferent exiles in the west
   Making love in cockney style.

Now the echoing palace fills;
   Men and women, girls and boys
Trample past the swords and frills,
   Kings and Queens and trulls and toys;
Or listening loll on window-sills,
   Happy amateurs of noise!

That for pictured rooms of state!
   Out they hurry, wench and knave,
Where beyond the palace-gate
   Dusty legions swarm and rave,
With laughter, shriek, inane debate,
   Kentish fire and comic stave.

Voices from the river call;
   Organs hammer tune on tune;
Larks triumphant over all
   Herald twilight coming soon,
For as the sun begins to fall
   Near the zenith gleams the moon.

From *The Testament of a Man Forbid*

Mankind has cast me out. When I became
So close a comrade of the day and night,
Of earth and of the seasons of the year,
And so submissive in my love of life
And study of the world that I unknew
The past and names renowned, religion, art,
Inventions, thoughts, and deeds, as men unknow
What good and evil fate befell their souls
Before their bodies gave them residence,
(How the old letter haunts the spirit still!
As if the soul were other than the sum
The body's powers make up – a golden coin,
Amount of so much silver, so much bronze!)
I said, rejoicing, 'Now I stand erect,
And am that which I am.' Compassionate
I watched a motley crowd beside me bent
Beneath unsteady burdens, toppling loads
Of volumes, news and lore antique, that showered
About their ears to be re-edified
On aching heads and shoulders overtasked.

Yet were these hodmen cheerful, ignorant
Of woe whose character it is to seem
Predestined and an honourable care:
They read their books, re-read, and read again;
They balanced libraries upon their polls,
And tottered through the valley almost prone,
But certain they were nobler than the beasts.
I saw besides in fields and cities hordes
Of haggard people soaked in filth and slime
Wherewith they fed the jaded earth the while
Their souls of ordure stank; automata
That served machines whose tyrannous revolt
Enthralled their lords, as if the mistletoe
Displaying mournful gold and wintry pearls
On sufferance, should enchant the forest oak
To be its accident and parasite;
Wretches and monsters that were capable
Of joy and sorrow once, their bodies numbed,
Their souls deflowered, their reason disendowed
By noisome trades, or at the furnaces,
In drains and quarries and the sunless mines;
And myriads upon myriads, human still
Without redemption drudging till they died.

Aware how multitudes of those enslaved
No respite sought, but squandered leisure hours
Among the crowd whose choice or task it was
To balance libraries upon their polls,
I laughed a long low laugh with weeping strung,
A rosary of tears, to see mankind
So dauntless and so dull, and cried at last,
'Good people, honest people, cast them off
And stand erect, for few are helped by books.
What! will you die crushed under libraries?
Lo! thirty centuries of literature
Have curved your spines and overborne your brains!
Off with it – all of it! Stand up; behold
The earth; life, death, and day and night!

Think not the things that have been said of these;
But watch them and be excellent, for men
Are what they contemplate.'

        They mocked me: 'Yah!
The fox who lost his tail! Though you are crazed
We have our wits about us.'

        'Nay,' I cried;
'There was besides an ape who lost his tail
That he might change to man. Undo the past!
The rainbow reaches Asgard now no more;
Olympus stands untenanted; the dead
Have their serene abode in earth itself,
Our womb, our nurture, and our sepulchre.
Expel the sweet imaginings, profound
Humanities and golden legends, forms
Heroic, beauties, tripping shades, embalmed
Through hallowed ages in the fragrant hearts
And generous blood of men; the climbing thoughts
Whose roots ethereal grope among the stars,
Whose passion-flowers perfume eternity,
Weed out and tear, scatter and tread them down;
Dismantle and dilapidate high heaven!
It has been said: Ye must be born again.
I say to you: Men must be that they are [. . . .]'

From *Holiday and Other Poems*

A Runnable Stag

When the pods went pop on the broom, green broom,
   And apples began to be golden-skinned,
We harboured a stag in the Priory coomb,
   And we feathered his trail up-wind, up-wind,
   We feathered his trail up-wind –
      A stag of warrant, a stag, a stag,
      A runnable stag, a kingly crop,
      Brow, bay and tray and three on top,
      A stag, a runnable stag.

Then the huntsman's horn rang yap, yap, yap,
   And 'Forwards' we heard the harbourer shout;
But 'twas only a brocket that broke a gap
   In the beechen underwood, driven out,
    From the underwood antlered out
      By warrant and might of the stag, the stag,
      The runnable stag, whose lordly mind
      Was bent on sleep, though beamed and tined
      He stood, a runnable stag.

So we tufted the covert till afternoon
   With Tinkerman's Pup and Bell-of-the-North;
And hunters were sulky and hounds out of tune
   Before we tufted the right stag forth,
    Before we tufted him forth,
      The stag of warrant, the wily stag,
      The runnable stag with his kingly crop,
      Brow, bay and tray and three on top,
      The royal and runnable stag.

It was Bell-of-the-North and Tinkerman's Pup
   That stuck to the scent till the copse was drawn.
'Tally ho! tally ho!' and the hunt was up,
   The tufters whipped and the pack laid on,
    The resolute pack laid on,
      And the stag of warrant away at last,
      The runnable stag, the same, the same,
      His hoofs on fire, his horns like flame,
      A stag, a runnable stag.

'Let your gelding be: if you check or chide
   He stumbles at once and you're out of the hunt;
For three hundred gentlemen, able to ride,
   On hunters accustomed to bear the brunt,
    Accustomed to bear the brunt,
      Are after the runnable stag, the stag,
      The runnable stag with his kingly crop,
      Bow, bay and tray and three on top,
      The right, the runnable stag.'

By perilous paths in coomb and dell,
  The heather, the rocks, and the river-bed,
The pace grew hot, for the scent lay well,
  And a runnable stag goes right ahead,
  The quarry went right ahead –
    Ahead, ahead, and fast and far;
    His antlered crest, his cloven hoof,
    Brow, bay and tray and three aloof,
    The stag, the runnable stag.

For a matter of twenty miles and more,
  By the densest hedge and the highest wall,
Through herds of bullocks he baffled the lore
  Of harbourer, huntsman, hounds and all,
  Of harbourer, hounds and all –
    The stag of warrant, the wily stag,
    For twenty miles, and five and five,
    He ran, and he never was caught alive,
    This stag, this runnable stag.

When he turned at bay in the leafy gloom,
  In the emerald gloom where the brook ran deep,
He heard in the distance the rollers boom,
  And he saw in a vision of peaceful sleep,
  In a wonderful vision of sleep,
    A stag of warrant, a stag, a stag,
    A runnable stag in a jewelled bed,
    Under the sheltering ocean dead,
    A stag, a runnable stag.

So a fateful hope lit up his eye,
  And he opened his nostrils wide again,
And he tossed his branching antlers high
  As he headed the hunt down the Charlock glen,
  As he raced down the echoing glen,
    For five miles more, the stag, the stag,
    For twenty miles, and five and five,
    Not to be caught now, dead or alive,
    The stag, the runnable stag.

Three hundred gentlemen, able to ride,
　　Three hundred horses as gallant and free,
Behind him escape on the evening tide,
　　Far out till he sank in the Severn Sea,
　　Till he sank in the depths of the sea –
　　　　The stag, the buoyant stag, the stag
　　　　That slept at last in a jewelled bed
　　　　Under the sheltering ocean spread,
　　　　The stag, the runnable stag.

From *The Testament of John Davidson*

The Last Journey

I felt the world a-spinning on its nave,
　　I felt it sheering blindly round the sun;
I felt the time had come to find a grave:
　　I knew it in my heart my days were done.
I took my staff in hand; I took the road,
And wandered out to seek my last abode.
　　　　Hearts of gold and hearts of lead
　　　　　Sing it yet in sun and rain,
　　　　'Heel and toe from dawn to dusk,
　　　　Round the world and home again.'

O long before the bere was steeped for malt,
　　And long before the grape was crushed for wine,
The glory of the march without a halt,
　　The triumph of a stride like yours and mine
Was known to folk like us, who walked about,
To be the sprightliest cordial out and out!
　　　　Folk like us, with hearts that beat,
　　　　　Sang it too in sun and rain –
　　　　'Heel and toe from dawn to dusk,
　　　　Round the world and home again.'

My feet are heavy now, but on I go,
   My head erect beneath the tragic years.
The way is steep, but I would have it so;
   And dusty, but I lay the dust with tears,
Though none can see me weep: alone I climb
The rugged path that leads me out of time –
         Out of time and out of all,
            Singing yet in sun and rain,
         'Heel and toe from dawn to dusk,
         Round the world and home again.'

Farewell the hope that mocked, farewell despair
   That went before me still and made the pace.
The earth is full of graves, and mine was there
   Before my life began, my resting-place;
And I shall find it out and with the dead
Lie down for ever, all my sayings said –
         Deeds all done and songs all sung,
            While others chant in sun and rain,
         'Heel and toe from dawn to dusk,
         Round the world and home again.'

From *Fleet Street and Other Poems*

from The Crystal Palace

Contraption, – that's the bizarre, proper slang,
Eclectic word, for this portentous toy,
The flying-machine, that gyrates stiffly, arms
A-kimbo, so to say, and baskets slung
From every elbow, skating in the air.
Irreverent, we; but Tartars from Thibet
May deem Sir Hiram the Grandest Lama, deem
His volatile machinery best, and most
Magnific, rotatory engine, meant
For penitence and prayer combined, whereby

Petitioner as well as orison
Are spun about in space: a solemn rite
Before the portal of that fane unique,
Victorian temple of commercialism,
Our very own eighth wonder of the world,
The Crystal Palace.

Prose Appendices

Ernest Dowson: 'To you, who are my verses. . .'
(From *Verses*, 1896)

In Preface: For Adelaide

To you, who are my verses, as on some very future day, if you ever care to read them, you will understand, would it not be somewhat trivial to dedicate any one verse, as I may do, in all humility, to my friends? Trivial, too, perhaps, only to name you even here? Trivial, presumptuous? For I need not write your name for you at least to know that this and all my work is made for you in the first place, and I need not to be reminded by my critics that I have no silver tongue such as were fit to praise you. So for once you shall go indedicate, if not quite anonymous; and I will only commend my little book to you in sentences far beyond my poor compass which will help you perhaps to be kind to it:

'*Votre personne, vos moindres mouvements me semblaient avoir dans le monde une importance extra-humaine. Mon cœur comme de la poussière se soulevait derrière vos pas. Vous me faisiez l'effet d'un clair-de-lune par une nuit d'été, quand tout est parfums, ombres douces, blancheurs, infini; et les délices de la chair et de l'âme étaient contenues pour moi dans votre nom que je me répétais en tachant de le baiser sur mes lèvres.*

'*Quelquefois vos paroles me reviennent comme un écho lointain, comme le son d'une cloche apporté par le vent; et il me semble que vous êtes là quand je lis des passages de l'amour dans les livres. . . . Tout ce qu'on y blâme d'exagéré, vous me l'avez fait ressentir.*'

Pont-Aven, Finistère, 1896

Lionel Johnson: On John Davidson

(From a letter to Katharine Tynan, later quoted by Ezra Pound in his Introduction to *The Poetical Works of Lionel Johnson*, 1915. It is also included by Iain Fletcher in his Textual Notes to *The Complete Poems of Lionel Johnson*, 1953.)

Powerful is the word, fervour, ardour, energy, rapid imagination and passion, sometimes heated and turbulent – a dash of Watson's sobriety would improve him. Intensely interested in *life* and its questions: a Scotch metaphysician turned into a romantic and realistic poet, without losing his *curiosity* about things. Versatile experimentalist, prolific: writes ballads, which are psychological problems dramatically conceived and put, with wonderful beauty of language at moments, but with a certain lack of delicacy – the poems rush and dash at you, overpower and invigorate you, rather than charm and enchant you. A restless poet – a true countryman of Burns and Carlyle, who has read the Elizabethans, and Keats and Browning. Earthy in a good sense; loves facts and Darwin: dreams and wonders and imagines, but always with a kind of robust consciousness. His beauty and his strength not in perfect accord. Take a poem of Watson; no amount of alteration would improve its decent and decorous mediocrity: Davidson's work often requires a last refining touch to transfigure it into a very wonderful thing. Hardest to estimate of all the younger poets: has tried so many ways and done so much. Has put genuine passion into his poetry, not an 'artistic' pose: full-blooded, generous, active: very human. Has not quite 'found himself' in literature or in life.

John Davidson: On Poetry

(From *A Rosary*, 1903)

Poetry is not always an army on parade: sometimes it is an army coming back from the wars, epaulettes and pipeclay all gone, shoeless, ragged, wounded, starved, but with victory on its brows; for Poetry has been democratized. Nothing could prevent that. The songs are of the highways and the byways. The city slums and the deserted villages are haunted by sorrowful figures, men of power and endurance, feeding their melancholy not with heroic fable, the beauty of the moon, and the studious cloisters, but with the actual sight of the misery in which so many millions live. To this mood the vaunted sweetness and light of the ineffective apostle of culture are, like a faded rose in a charnel-house, a flash of moonshine on the Dead Sea. It is not now to the light that 'the passionate heart of the poet' will turn. The poet is in the street, the hospital. He intends the world to know it is out of joint. He will not let it alone. Democracy is here; and we have to go through with it. The newspaper is one of the most potent forces in moulding the character of contemporary poetry. Burns's eyes were open; Blake's, perhaps, for a time; and Wordsworth had profound insight into the true character of man and the world; but all the rest saw men as trees walking; Tennyson and Browning are Shakespearian. The prismatic cloud that Shakespeare hung out between poets and the world! It was the newspapers that brought about what may be called an order of pre-Shakespearianism. It was in the newspapers that Thomas Hood found the 'Song of the Shirt' – in its place the most important English poem of the nineteenth century; the 'woman in unwomanly rags plying her needle and thread' is the type of the world's misery. The 'Song of the Shirt' is the most terrible poem in the English language. Only a high heart and strong brain broken on the wheel of life, but master of its own pain and anguish, able to jest in the jaws of death, could have sung this song, of which every single stanza wrings the heart. Poetry passed by on the other side. It could not endure the woman in unwomanly rags. It hid its head like the fabled ostrich in some sand-bed of Arthurian legend, or took shelter in the paradoxical optimism of 'The Ring and the Book'. It is true William Morris stood by her when the priest and the Levite passed by. He stood by her side, he helped her; but he hardly saw her, nor could he show her as she is. 'Mother and Son', his greatest poem, and a very great poem, is a vision not of a woman, but of a deserted Titaness in London streets; there was a veil between him also and the world, although in another sense, with his elemental Sigurds, he is the truest of all pre-Shakespearians. But the woman in unwomanly rags, and all the insanity and iniquity of which she is the type, will now be sung. Poetry will concern itself with her and hers for some time to come. Not much of the harlot: she is at ease in Zion compared with actual woe. The offal of the world is being said in statistics, in prose fiction; it is besides going to be sung. There it is in the streets, the hospitals, the poor-houses, the prisons; it is a flood that surges about our feet, it rises breast-high, and it will be sung in all keys and voices. Poetry has other functions, other aims; but this also has become its province.